Fertility Follies

Adventures In
Hormones & Hot Flashes

Fertility Follies

Adventures In
Hormones & Hot Flashes

. . . .

Erin Miserlis

Fertility Follies — Adventures In Hormones & Hot Flashes
Copyright © 2013 by Erin Miserlis

Edited by Tao Stadler
Book cover design and illustration by Petro Design Co.
Photography by Rebecca Cameron

ISBN 978-0-9913597-0-7

To Peter —
for teaching me to stop talking and start doing
and for never giving up.

To Theo and Stefania —
you made my life, you were worth it all.

Finally, to my own Mother Stephanie, who introduced me
to the joy of books and with her great laugh, taught me how to
love.

What Readers Have Said About

Fertility Follies

Adventures In Hormones & Hot Flashes

"Reading this book was like sitting down with Erin for a series of wonderful conversations. Her storytelling skills are remarkable, full of love and grace, humor, irony and sublime wisdom. I will share this brilliant book with friends, family and clients."
– Liza Boyer, LCSW, La Jolla CA

"I loved this book! I read it in two days because it felt like I was having a conversation with a new, but soon to be good friend who had also dealt with infertility. Erin's story banishes the isolation often associated with infertility, while offering practical suggestions for coping with your own struggles. Her humor will help get you through that lunch date with your 8

months pregnant friend, who confides dramatically about her 3 month turmoil trying to conceive, all the while rubbing her stomach and telling you to just relax and stop thinking about it!"

– Sue Crooks, Registered Nurse, 4-year navigator of the infertility highway, and mother of Madelyn thanks to IVF

*"You will laugh, you will cry, you will find hope, and you will realize you are not alone as Erin shares her journey so openly and honestly! This is a **MUST READ** for anyone experiencing the despair, confusion and mystery of infertility."*

– Tracy Johnson, Licensed Therapist, Infertility Survivor, Mother of 2 sons (biological & adopted)

"FINALLY there is a book that I can relate to! Fertility Follies takes the reader through the challenging journey of infertility and loss with the author's heartfelt, yet at times humorous, explanation. I was laughing, crying, and sighing all along the way. Erin openly shares her experiences and personal struggles. From the devastating losses, costly infertility treatments, raging hormones, to the internal emotional battles, and the jealousy of others who attain motherhood so easily. I could feel her heartache and determination and for a moment, thought I was reading my own diary. If you are struggling with infertility and/or loss, this book will show you that you are absolutely NOT alone. It

will encourage you to open your heart to hope. Dreams really do come true!"

– Christi Treibach — Infertility Survivor and mother of twins

"Witty and charming, yet tenderly open and honest, this invigorating ride on Erin's personal fertility roller coaster left me laughing, crying, and truly touched by her genuine gift for finding humor in even the darkest places. Erin shows us not only that we aren't alone in our quests to begin or add to our families, but that finding a way to embrace this difficult road can perhaps be one of the greatest gifts of all."

– Jeneanne Paden, L.Ac. — Acupuncture Fertility Center

Author's Note

This book is based on the author's interpretation of her experience with infertility. Hormone inducing drugs and authors license may have had an effect on storytelling, but to the best of her knowledge all details are correct. In some cases, names and/or locations have been changed to protect privacy.

This Is Bigger Than Money

A portion of proceeds from the sale of each book will be contributed to the "This is Bigger Than Money Fund" to help supplement the costs of alternative treatments for individuals coping with infertility. The fund is a direct result of the caring services provided by Jeneanne Paden, L.Ac. and the staff at the Acupuncture Fertility Center in San Diego, California.

Table of Contents

HI

Chapter 1

Kitchens &
Conversations

This book began in a kitchen. Completely appropriate considering I would ultimately spend over three years in and out of doctors offices, hospitals, and clinics trying out every new pharmaceutical recipe to make a baby of my own. I was the epitome of the watched pot that never boiled, hopelessly stuck in a never-ending cycle of waiting.

Worn out from swimming through the abyss of infertility, I was at a loss for what to do next. With each disappointment, it became that much harder to rationalize my failed attempts at becoming a mother. I was out of excuses and forced to face the reality that I might never give birth to a child of my own. A positive pregnancy test no longer represented the magic of parenthood, only a debilitating fear of a miscarriage. For one gleaming second the excitement of pregnancy would surround me, only to be overshadowed by the larger presence of loss. I was doing my best to hide it, but I was scared to find myself becoming angry and bitter.

I was feeling increasingly alone and having a hard time being around pregnant women or people with babies. Instead of honoring my pregnant friends, I began to avoid them. I preferred to stay in my bubble of denial, hiding from any baby centered events that weren't hosted by an MD. I built a warped emotional wall that only allowed me to be happy for those who had struggled with at least some form of infertility. I found it especially hard to cope when someone became pregnant without really trying, fresh off birth control and already counting the days to delivery. How could I celebrate such a pregnancy when I was tracking years of trying instead of gestational weeks?

The unfairness weighed down on me and I was unable to stop the negativity from flowing within. I had forgotten how to view a child as a gift and could only see them as a right. I fixated on why I felt other people shouldn't have children, unable to get past my inability to have one of my own. A friend whose husband had an affair became pregnant shortly after their reconciliation. I was irate that someone who had disrespected their family could have a child so easily. Without warning I cut off the friendship, leaving my friend sitting in a wake of bewilderment at my sudden abandonment.

I seemed to be surrounded by pregnant people and they became unavoidable reminders as to what I couldn't have. Despite my best efforts, there was nothing more that I could do. I had to be content with sitting back and watching as every smoker, user, or teenager around me wound up pregnant. I began to contemplate the benefits of becoming a crack addict. According to the news it was quite the fertility drug. Not a bad option considering the only buzz I'd had in months was from the pain killers handed out after each miscarriage. What fun is that if you are confined to a bed, sleeping through it all? Compared to In Vitro Fertilization, crack was starting to sound like a much more reasonable alternative and for a fraction of the cost.

I was ashamed of myself yet I couldn't stop these feelings. Envy towards the fertility blessed was as much of a part of my life as trying to conceive. Sometimes I would learn of another person's struggle with infertility and secretly I'd feel a glimmer of gratification, because for once, I wasn't alone. This sick sense of self-preservation was new to me and growing darker as each passing month pushed me that much farther away from becoming a mother. These thoughts were swirling around in my head as I tried to move forward and live my life without the constant companion of infertility by my side.

During this time, I was working at a non-profit agency where my office was a converted storage closet outfitted with fluorescent lighting and thick, white brick walls. Sitting in my windowless box, I would often find myself in need of a jolt of sunshine. Late in the afternoon I would gravitate towards the communal kitchen for some light therapy and human interaction. It was in that kitchen that a conversation about the frustration of dealing with infertility and the premise of this book began.

As with most kitchens, ours was a place of conversation. It was there during these self-imposed sunlight breaks that I met Tracy. With similar interests, our kitchen conversations slowly turned into lunches and a friendship was formed. Being women in our thirties our biological clocks had long been ringing, and children were often the topic of discussion. Tracy was the first person I met who was also dealing with infertility. It had taken her over a year to get pregnant and she was devastated when that pregnancy ended in a miscarriage. Our friendship deepened over our shared loss, and having the opportunity to talk with someone without fear of judgment was an integral part of normalizing my destructive feelings. My husband, Peter, was extremely supportive, yet as women it is our bodies that provide us with a monthly update and undeniable proof of our failure. For the partner, no matter how involved, there isn't that constant reminder or second-guessing of every feeling inside our bodies. It is hard to let go and live your life normally with the incessant monitoring that is such an overwhelming part of the fertility process.

Shortly into my fertility follies, I was starting to sense that in spite of my doctor's reassurances, getting pregnant might not be that easy. My second miscarriage woke me to the reality of infertility, and I was beginning to grasp that I had no control over my fertility. Leaning towards obsessive tendencies helped create the mental façade I needed to move forward, and I started to become unnaturally obsessed with the calendar. My calendar stalking was the first sign that maybe I was having a harder time dealing with my infertility than I had realized. The stalking begins with counting the days until you ovulate. I had a thick black Sharpie that I would use to mark the days until ovulation, which I then signaled by drawing a big giant circle around the date. Looking at my calendar, one would think the date represented a vacation or a special event, not a visual status of my menstrual cycle.

Once ovulation occurs, the counting starts again, this time focusing on the earliest date possible to take a pregnancy test. By now, I would have convinced myself that every gas pain or twitch was a sign of pregnancy. My breasts were larger, definitely larger because I was pregnant, not because I had spent the past month stress eating my way through it. The concept of the EPT (early pregnancy test) must have been created with fertility challenged women in mind. What other kind of person would want to take a pregnancy test so soon? I am convinced the company realized the EPT was a creative way to make an additional buck, because if the test comes up negative you tell yourself that you must be testing too early. You continue to take a test each day until it becomes painfully obvious that you aren't pregnant, just down a hundred bucks in your checking account.

I am embarrassed to say that on more than one occasion I woke up at 4:00 a.m. and couldn't resist the temptation to take a test. Peter would be sleeping quietly, completely oblivious as I stood in the dark in my underwear waiting patiently for the blue line to appear. He would see the results in the trash in the morning and ask me why I was torturing myself again, why couldn't I just wait until my period was late? I was never able to get him to understand that waiting made it worse. The anticipation was dreadful, my imagination would run wild as I spent every second mentally debating whether I was pregnant or not. It was all consuming and I couldn't think of anything else. Testing kept my mind occupied and made me feel as if I actively had some sense of control over my fertility. The manic counting would resume as soon as I got my period. Another date marked with a black circle, another month of counting. Staring at the calendar and predicting the dates of ovulation, predicting the date of when I could begin testing, and sneaking in enough hope to make me do it all over again, month after month after month.

With Tracy, I was able to be myself and didn't have to be afraid of the crazed image that I had become. We laughed away many difficult days discussing our newfound appreciation of the quickie, or whether or not porn was okay for the sake of fertility. Most people don't realize that by the time you are engaging in doctor prescribed sex, there is nothing sexy about it. One of the many words of advice given to me during this time was to remember that the best part about babies was making them. Clearly they had never been instructed by their doctor to go home and have mechanical sex with their partner, finish it off by keeping your legs motionless in the air, and by all means, refrain from using the bathroom. This is of course assuming you are still having sex with your partner and not a Petri dish. What fun is sex with all of these rules and stipulations? I hadn't had this much instruction since my first time!

As with every difficult time in life, there are always bright spots. I associate these days with sadness and loss, but as odd as it sounds with a lot of laughter. Second to Peter, Tracy was my constant companion during this time. She was the first person I called when I found out I had *accidentally* gotten pregnant just prior to starting my second round of In-Vitro. I called her while sitting on the floor inside of my bedroom closet. It was the only place I felt safe enough to say the words, "I'm pregnant." She was truly happy for me, just as I was for her, when she found out she was pregnant a month later.

This book is for everyone who doesn't have a Tracy, people who think they are alone and going crazy with the madness of infertility. I have been there and I understand those nights in the dark in your underwear, and yes, sometimes that blue line really does appear.

STERILE

Chapter ❷

Insanity,
Utter Insanity

The only time my husband ever cheated on me was with a cup. After my third miscarriage my doctor sat me down and said, "I think you have a problem." Somehow I knew he wasn't referring to my habit of hiding Nordstrom sales receipts. He gave me a referral for a fertility specialist and sent me on my way. It was official, I had a problem and along with it, validation for what I had been feeling for months. Strange as it sounds, I was excited about meeting the specialist. I foolishly expected some magic concoction would be taking me from the hormonal highway to the carpool lane in no time at all.

After a series of tests, tests, and more tests, it was decided that I would begin a trial of the fertility drug Clomid and pair it with an IUI, a fancy word for the turkey-baster method. The acronym stands for Intrauterine Insemination, but I think Insanity Utter Insanity is much more appropriate. If I thought I was crazy before, this new phase in my fertility follies made me eligible for full time residency in an asylum. I know that Clomid has been a wonder drug for many people and by all means I am not disputing its effectiveness, but for me Clomid was probably the worst part of all my treatments. Considering I was to become a human version of a lab rat, this says a lot. What I thought to be an insignificant little daily pill was actually an oral inferno. No one told me that one of the many unpleasant side effects was hot flashes. Horrible, long, coming all day and soaking your bed into the night, kind of hot flashes. I am breaking into a post-traumatic sweat just thinking about it.

The building I worked at while being treated for infertility didn't have air conditioning, so it became a regular occurrence to see me in the break room with my head stuck in the freezer. Not a good image to project considering I was working at a crisis prevention center. All I can say is at least it wasn't an oven. A sweaty upper lip was just the beginning of my concerns. Along with the warning for an increase in multiple births should have been one about multiple personalities. Sybil had nothing on me and I pity those few brave souls who tried to point out any changes in my behavior. Short tempered, emotional, sweaty, and growing plumper by the day, I was a vague representation of my former self. Sadly, the only new addition to our family was my Clomid induced personality.

My doctor assured me this was normal and we moved forward with part two, the IUI. This is when Peter's love affair with the cup really began. The main component of an IUI involves taking a sample from the male (For Peter's pride, I'll let you figure this one out on your own), giving it a wash to get rid of anything less than the baby making material (I prefer to think of this as grooming for the big date), and then returning the sample to its given destination (what else can I say, his Mom is reading this after all) with the help of an extra long tube. No disrespect to any of the males, the length helps ensure the sample gets a first class ride directly to the uterus. Quite the process for something so simple.

During our consultation, we were given very strict instructions from the nurse. The sample had to be collected at home at a specific time, brought back to the office for the wash, and the transfer happened shortly thereafter. We were handed an unobtrusive brown paper bag that held a small specimen cup and sent on our way. Knowing that in a few short hours this sack could very well be our child's first home made my head spin. I couldn't help but think that if the procedure worked, how would I feel telling my child their first few moments on Earth were in a paper bag? Even worse, how would they feel knowing what their dad did to get them there?

The collection aspect of the treatment process can become quite stressful for the male. We all know that masturbation is a part of life, but I really don't want to know when my husband is taking care of business. To make matters worse, once you are handed that paper sack the doctors, nurses, and everyone else in that office, know exactly what you will be doing in a few hours. Even with eyes averted, it is a long walk back to the clinic parking lot. Performance anxiety is a natural reaction to this sort of scenario and considering that there is also a hefty price tag attached to each procedure, the amount of stress is only elevated.

When dealing with infertility, many males can internalize their inability to impregnate their partners as somehow attributed to a lack in their manhood. A perfect example of this is a story shared with me by our nurse. We were discussing how intrusive the IUI process is and considering males haven't been indoctrinated with a life of annual trips to the Gyno, seeing a doctor can be a very nerve wracking experience. Living in San Diego, we have two pro sports team on hand. One very famous athlete (name withheld for the sake of a future playoff game), had to come out to his doctor about double dipping. Apparently when he submitted his sample he decided it didn't appear to be large enough and he took it upon himself to add a second round for good measure. When the sample was analyzed the sperm count was so diluted they thought he might have a problem. Embarrassed, he had to admit what he did. As you can see, there is no gender bias in IUI insanity.

I was relentless in teasing Peter about his role in the IUI. Inside the paper sack was a wonderful little cup. This cup was forever to be known as the other plastic woman. As with most fertility treatments there was no sex for us, but the cup was sure to get plenty of action. I toyed with making the moment meaningful by decorating the cup with girlie pictures, but didn't think the staff back at the clinic would look too kindly at that. Instead, I tried to set the scene by dancing around seductively when handing Peter his morning coffee. In my best B movie actress voice, I'd ask if the cup made him horny. Forget leaving me for another woman, I now had a whole cabinet to worry about.

On the morning of his big submission, I brought Peter the cup in my cleavage. I don't know if this helped or horrified him, but it was all I could do. A result of our doctor prescribed sex, this so called foreplay was of a completely different realm. We had moved on to a new level in baby making, and with it so did my sense of humor. At least we were laughing again. The big day had arrived and it was time to put our paper bag and the other plastic woman to use. As I drove to the clinic, I couldn't decide between seat-belting the paper bag in place or keeping it in my purse. I thought my purse might get too hot, or god-forbid, the sample could spill. I opted for an early lesson in child safety and buckled it in. I drove extra slow, hoping I wouldn't get pulled over by the police and explain the questionable looking bag on the adjacent seat.

I began to wonder if it would help my chances if I romanced the doctor. Should I be bringing the nurse flowers? What about candles and wine? Will I get a call tomorrow or is this just a new fangled booty call? I had the warped sense that if I created a scene of seduction maybe my success rate would be higher. The doctor would be wowed by my charms and we'd get to throw in an extra sample for good luck. Here I was about to make a baby, and my husband wasn't even going to be in the room. I don't know about you, but in my book that is called an affair. Somehow this wasn't the way I had envisioned bringing my child into the world. First Peter cheats on me with the cup and now I am about to have a new-age threesome with my doctor. It can't get any worse than this, but I guess fair is fair, let the insanity begin.

Chapter ③

Miscarriage of Justice

The first time I miscarried I thought it was a fluke, the second time I attributed it to bad luck, the third time I was scared, and the fourth time can only be described as a miscarriage of justice. I had been married for two years, had the house, the dog, the SUV and according to the American Dream, the baby was supposed to be next. Peter and I had nonchalantly made the decision to become parents. With our life in place, everyone assumed the next step would be children, and so did we.

It took a few attempts at giving up birth control before I was finally able to break up with Ortho Novum for good. Peter and I spent months deliberating over the right time to build a family until we had exhausted the conversation, and ran out of reasons for waiting any longer. I was scared about what having a baby would require, but blindly moved on towards this next phase in our life. Eight months later I was pregnant, and I found myself watching a television commercial promoting youth literacy. Sitting in my less than kid-friendly living room, it suddenly dawned on me, we weren't just going to have a baby, we were going to be parents. The realization that for the rest of my life I was to be responsible for another person's existence was terrifying. There was no turning back and I sat in silence slightly panicking over my impending motherhood.

A few days later I miscarried. Peter and I had been getting ready to meet some friends for dinner when I noticed some light spotting. I read in my pregnancy book that this can happen during implantation when the fertilized egg attaches to the lining of the uterus. Momentarily relieved, we opted to skip dinner and stay home for the evening. It wasn't long before the spotting turned to bleeding, and we decided to go to the local E.R. for reassurance. When the doctor told me the pregnancy was terminating, I stared at him blankly, unable to fully absorb what he was telling me. I was so new to the realm of infertility that I didn't understand a trip to the hospital didn't equate to a cure. I couldn't believe there wasn't anything they could do. The flow of blood meant nothing to me, mentally I was still pregnant.

What shocked me most was the immediate stinging sense of loss that I felt. Any doubts I'd had about becoming a parent were erased with that first miscarriage. No longer having the option, I realized I truly was ready, and I wanted a baby more than anything. Even though I was only pregnant a short while, I had already started to envision our new life. I had to say goodbye not just to the baby, but to the dream of what the baby and eventually our family, would have become. It is hard to describe the deep sense of loss you feel when you lose a pregnancy. Although not quite a child, each pregnancy carries its own dreams and memories, and however short, their absence requires a grieving process all of their own. Peter and I were both sad, but we tried to look at the miscarriage as a gift. Gone were any lingering doubts about having children and with this newfound security we were eager to try again.

After losing that first pregnancy, I learned that on average about 1 in 5 end in miscarriage. Some experts speculate that number to be much higher with women mistaking an early miscarriage for a late, but very heavy period. I was young and healthy and there was no obvious reason as to why I shouldn't be able to conceive again. Having hit my 1 in 5 so early, I had the naïve confidence of a woman who'd already been a statistic. I was so sure of myself that the next time I was pregnant I told everyone around me. The possibility of another miscarriage was the outermost thing from my mind. When it happened again my doctor said not to worry, this was nothing more than bad luck. This one hurt, it hurt my heart, my body, and my resolve. I began to secretly wonder if maybe my doctor was wrong, maybe there was more to this than bad luck. To top it off, I was embarrassed. In my excited haste I prematurely shared my news with everyone around me. I had to face friends and neighbors and go back to work when all I really wanted to do was stay in bed and hide.

Returning to work was always met with a sense of finality. Outwardly, this was the last step in grieving the pregnancy. My body had healed and I had come down from the immediate crisis of the situation. Returning to a normal life and my old routine proved to be nothing more than a blatant reminder of how abnormal I was feeling. Dodging the sympathetic glances of well meaning co-workers did nothing other than make me want to retreat with shame for something I couldn't control. My doctor said I was fine, so I must be. Despite how I felt on the inside, my return to work was the end of my socially acceptable pity party. Time to move on, whether you are ready to or not.

My third pregnancy I chose to be more discreet. I told just a few close friends and only those who needed to know at work. I was much more cautious and rarely left the house. I wanted more than anything to put myself into a cocoon for the next 12 weeks and wake up when my first trimester was over. I began to doubt the success of my pregnancy. Every trip to the bathroom was met with fear as I would obsessively check for any signs of blood. The excitement that a new pregnancy brings was forever lost on me as I anticipated the worst. I was trying hard to remain hopeful, but the insecurity of infertility was beginning to take over. I was entering a dark phase in my fertility follies, which unbeknownst to me was going to last years.

By my third miscarriage I knew what to expect. I awoke late one night with a cramping sensation and immediately knew what was happening. I watched as my husband slept and I couldn't bring myself to wake him. Waking him would make this real. I fooled myself into thinking if I could just go back to sleep my body would shut down and put an end to what was happening. I lay there in numb silence willing everything to stop. I stared at Peter's face in the dark and thought of the secret that I was holding inside. I knew what waking him would bring. Let him have this just a little bit longer. The peacefulness of his sleep keeping the impending nightmare at bay.

After my third miscarriage, I was officially diagnosed with Unexplainable Recurrent Pregnancy Loss. This is nothing more than a polite way of saying they have no idea what is wrong with you, and I was referred to a fertility specialist. I let myself get excited again, being trained in fertility issues, I was sure my new doctor would have some higher knowledge not passed on to the mere mortal OBGYN's. I was in awe of my doctor, feeling that he held the answer to all of my problems and if I did what I was told, I would get my lollypop reward of a smiling, chubby baby. Being new to the world of diagnosed infertility, there was a wealth of options ahead of me and I was eager to start sampling them all.

The path to parenthood required additional testing for both Peter and I, and it wasn't until close to a year of treatment before I finally became pregnant again. The enthusiasm I had shown during my initial phase of treatment had waned to an equal level of bitterness and frustration. The specialist was supposed to fix me, not make things worse. I'd gone from being an incompetent but fertile patient, to one who wasn't even able to tell when she was ovulating. I underwent eight months of Clomid induced cycles without any success. All I got out of it was water weight and an ability to sweat on command. My hormones were racing at a dizzying pace and I was losing faith that I'd ever give birth to a biological child.

The doctor suggested we try the more aggressive route of an IUI (Intrauterine Insemination), where a sperm sample is collected and with the help of a catheter, the sperm is placed directly into the uterus, reducing the amount of travel time. The shorter the distance, the better chance at fertilization, and I was thrilled to find out I was pregnant after my second attempt. I felt that all of my hard work had finally paid off and prayed that this pregnancy would stick. The specialist was my last option, my fertility god, and I couldn't handle it if another miscarriage knocked him off his pedestal. I put everything I had left into convincing myself that this pregnancy would work, and was absolutely crushed when I miscarried again.

I was devastated and spiraled into a place of inescapable anger and self pity. Was there no justice? I asked myself over and over why this kept happening and I could never find the answer. I lived my life based on the premise that if you were a good person, good things happened to you. How could I continue to believe this when I was stuck at some absurd end of an unbalanced scale for no fault of my own? This pregnancy loss shook not only my belief in my ability to become a parent, but my outlook on the world in general. My miscarriage of justice ruined me emotionally and spiritually, and I had no way of knowing how to get it back.

It was around this time that one of my best friends was diagnosed with cervical cancer. I had met Nikki during my first month away at college. We bonded over an afternoon of cheap beer and tubing down the local river. We started a conversation that to this day has never ended. Nikki's health crisis helped put my life in perspective; whatever I was going through was rough, but I had to remind myself, was voluntary. In fact, I had often wondered about the location of the fertility clinic I attended. Part of a major hospital, it was directly adjacent to the oncology department. Each week as I took the elevator to the second floor, I would be joined by a variety of people, young and old, in varying degrees of illness. Here I was struggling to create a life, when all around me were people fighting just to keep the one they had. This blatant reminder, paired with Nikki's illness, helped teach me to be grateful for what I had.

One of the things that Nikki and I shared was a love of running. She had given me a pair of running socks the last time we'd gotten together. With Nikki in mind, I wore them to the hospital for my scheduled D&C. Although the pregnancy was no longer viable, my body was still retaining the pregnancy. The D&C procedure would help remove the remaining tissue and allow the healing process to begin. Even though I'd been through this surgery numerous times before, it never got any easier. I knew the pregnancy had self terminated, but the medicinal cleansing of my body was an unwelcome and harsh method of forced closure. Always anxious, I would have a nurse hold my hand as I was wheeled down the corridor for those last few minutes before I was sent adrift in consciousness. This time I looked at the socks on my feet, closed my eyes, and reminded myself of what they represented. I was alive, I was not sick, and I was going to be okay. Nikki's symbolic feet inspired me to get back on my own, and back on with my life.

Continuing with treatment never got any easier, but as I'd find myself slipping into negativity, Nikki's feet were always there to kick me along. A tangible reminder of all the things I still had to be thankful for. I don't believe that there will ever be a balance for infertility. We can never anticipate what is around the corner or why life takes the turns that it does. Years later, when I had my son, he arrived wild and smiling. Full of confidence, he has had our attention from day one. Seeing him now it all makes sense, his personality is so full of life that he was destined to be the baby that made it. I wouldn't wish those years on anyone, but maybe, just maybe, there is justice after all.

Chapter ❹

Alternative Routes

I am embarrassed to say I got the idea from an episode of Sex and the City. Well, not entirely, but almost. A friend had originally proposed acupuncture to me after my third miscarriage. He had recently graduated from medical school and was specializing in Eastern Medicine and said I should give acupuncture a try. I assumed it was better suited for new age hippies and being a lifelong needle-phobe, the idea of getting willingly poked with not one, but hundreds of needles didn't sound like my idea of fun. I shrugged the suggestion off and added it to my pile of unsolicited, useless advice such as just relax, and moved on.

I had been seeing a fertility specialist and was thrilled to find out I was pregnant after my second attempt at an IUI. The ultrasound didn't bring good news. The baby's heartbeat was extremely low and it was more than likely I would miscarry again. The doctor said there was nothing I could do other than go home, get some rest and wait. I sat around my house trying not to think of the inevitable. It was around this time that I saw the episode of Sex and the City where one of the characters tries acupuncture and gets pregnant. I was desperate and willing to try anything, even needles. Remembering my friend's advice, I did an internet search on acupuncture and up popped a wealth of information.

One of the first pages that came up had a photo of a smiling woman named Jeneanne, who looked nice and more importantly, like she wouldn't get much enjoyment out of poking people with needles. On her website was a study published in an issue of *Fertility and Sterility* that found when pairing IVF (In Vitro Fertilization) with acupuncture, the success rate jumps from **26.3% to 42.5%.** It got me thinking that maybe it could help patients in my situation who were suffering from repeated pregnancy loss. I took a deep breath and sent an email requesting information. With one click of the mouse I was on my way to becoming a crystal wearing, Birkenstock loving, new age disciple.

The email turned into a phone call and Jeneanne patiently answered all of my questions. Having such a weak heartbeat it was medically impossible for that baby to survive, but Jeneanne still took the time to talk with me. She recognized my desperate need for emotional support and despite the hopeless diagnosis, provided some much needed encouragement. I eventually lost the baby but we remained in touch.

A few months later when I was getting ready to try another insemination, Jeneanne suggested I come in for a consultation. I nervously accepted and the whole way to my appointment I couldn't help but think why was I doing this? I hated needles, and hated everything about how intrusive this fertility process was, yet here I was about to add another layer to my treatments. More poking, more prodding, and of course, more money. Yet for some reason, I still showed up to my appointment.

I nervously sat in the examination room and silently laughed at myself. As I had expected, there was the prerequisite smell of incense and hippie music playing in the background. My palms were sweating and I thought about heading out the door more than once. Thankfully Jeneanne appeared and we began the appointment by looking at the needles. They were small, not as big as I'd imagined, and I was happy to learn that only a small part would actually penetrate the skin. First she poked herself (okay so maybe she was a little more sadistic than I thought) and then she asked if I was ready. She gently inserted the first needle into the top of my hand. Surprisingly, I felt nothing, absolutely nothing, and it was great! With my needle fears put to rest we decided to go ahead with the rest of the appointment. I was told to expect a little pressure in the uterus area and that was about it. I felt like superwoman and needles were no longer my kryptonite. I happily stripped down, plopped up on the table, and got ready for the baby making to commence.

After so many pain filled months, I was taking control of my fertility and it was nice to feel hopeful again. The placement process didn't take very long, fifteen minutes at most. While inserting the needles, Jeneanne told me we were also going to try some guided mental imagery. This was supposed to help encourage the development of the potential fetus by using positive energy. I always resisted the usefulness of guided mental imagery, and in college when studying psychology, I had used it as free nap time instead. I could feel the patchouli-oiled believers in the world unite as I realized there was no escaping this new-agey exercise, and I mumbled in uncomfortable agreement.

I was instructed to close my eyes and beginning with my toes, imagine my body welcoming a new spirit into my womb. I was doing my best not to laugh and stay open to the experience. What did I have to lose? I was already so far beyond my comfort zone that there was no use in turning back. As hard as I tried, the only image I could come up with was a mini apron-wearing version of myself, standing outside my uterus with a warm plate saying, "Come on in new little life, I have cookies." This was the most welcoming vision I could conjure up and I was hoping it would work. Any kid of mine would be genetically predisposed to an obsession with sweets, so I prayed this vision was enticing enough.

After the imagery session, Jeneanne explained that she would leave me in the room to allow the energy to flow through my body. I was to stay on the table and try to relax. Considering there was a box's worth of needles sticking out of me, there wasn't much else I could do. It must have been about 5 minutes before I felt some pressure. Shockingly, the acupuncture was giving me the same sensation felt in my uterus while taking Clomid, except this was completely natural. Suddenly the pressure became a bit stronger and I realized it was making me feel as if I had to go to the bathroom. I wasn't worried; surely Jeneanne would be back at any moment. I tried to listen to the hippie music to distract my mind. The pressure began to increase and I got a little uncomfortable. More hippie music, more pressure. With each song the pressure increased and suddenly I realized I was sweating. I'd never had to pee this bad in my life. I felt like I'd just drunk a gallon of water, a six-pack of beer, and a pot of coffee all in one sitting. I had to pee so bad it hurt. I started to shift around on the table and it took all my willpower to hold it in.

Someone was punishing me for a lifetime of making fun of hippie music because now it was all I could focus on. Enya was now the musical soundtrack to my mental chant of, "Don't pee Enya, don't pee Enya." Forget welcoming the fetus with cookies, I was now moving on to a bathroom. "Hello little friend, not only will I have cookies, I'll also have a big clean bathroom with a Jacuzzi tub that I promise never to make you clean." The songs dragged on and I was sweating profusely. I was about to sweat pee because I had to go so bad. Suddenly the music changed to nature sounds; oh no, not a waterfall, anything but a waterfall. I change my mind, Jeneanne really is sadistic, she likes poking people and she's probably hiding somewhere laughing at this very minute. I was at the point of no return and was about to pee all over myself and her beautiful incense scented examination room. I couldn't take it any longer, I had to get up and find a bathroom. I tried to stand, but immediately felt as if I was being held down. The energy from the acupuncture was so strong that I couldn't get up. I was stuck, literally and figuratively and there was nothing I could do about it.

I began to call her name, Jeneanne, Jeneanne once or twice, quiet and soft until finally my pleas became stronger and more repetitive. Jeneanne, Jeneanne became Jeneannnnnnnnnnnne, accompanied by a few kicks on the table for good measure. Finally, she came in the room and I burst out, "I have to Peeeeeee!!" She pulled the needles out of me as fast as she could, while trying to suppress a laugh. If Jeneanne could hear me from outside the room, I am sure all of the other patients did too. Intruding on their mental Zen was my whining voice screaming like a banshee. I am pretty sure I scared away a few new patients that day. I was proof that you did indeed feel those needles, why else would someone be screaming like that? I half-heartedly threw on a gown and dashed through the waiting room to the bathroom. If the other patients didn't hear my cries, they sure did hear my, "Ahhhhhhhhhhh."

Once settled back in the examination room, I couldn't hide my embarrassment. Jeneanne was quick to assure me that this happened all the time. Despite this, in the subsequent year I spent visiting her office, I never did see a streaking pee'er run through the waiting room. We came up with a system after that, Jeneanne would leave me with a bell and if rung, she'd come running. It never happened again, but thankfully this experience allowed me to let go of any awkwardness I had with asking questions or trying out new procedures, even a little guided mental imagery. If I could survive flashing a room full of complete strangers and almost peeing all over myself, then inviting a fake baby in for cookies was going to be a piece of cake.

Chapter ⑤

All is Fair in Love and Fertility

Just as all is fair in love and war, the same can be said for fertility. Every day, normally sane people willingly sign up for surgery and agree to poke themselves with needles, just for a chance at beating infertility. I never would have believed the only kind of elective surgery I'd have wasn't going to involve some sort of nip or tuck. If doctors really suspect a link between stress levels and infertility, they should consider combining IVF packages with a few cosmetic options. If I can't end up with a teenage daughter, then I should at least get the perky breasts of one. Thousands of surgical dollars and not a thing to show for it. I could inject myself better than a junkie, but was never given the pleasure of even a minute of drug-induced euphoria. Yet, like an addict, I always came back for more.

People dealing with infertility share a unique bond. Social lines become blurred as we seek a sense of camaraderie amongst our peers. Complete strangers commiserate over hot flashes, pregnancy envy, and surprisingly their sex lives. At this point, the process for making a baby is so far removed from anything sexual that we become desensitized to the entire process. Suddenly, discussing my husband masturbating into a cup is socially acceptable conversation, and calling a friend post ovulation night and asking, "How did it go?" is merely an attempt at being supportive. A very adult problem reduces people to talking about sex like teenagers.

I knew more about some of my friends' ovulation cycles than I did my own. My friend Tracy and I were typically about a week apart. It wasn't until she called me upset over getting her period that I realized I was late for my own. Completely unaware that I was pregnant, I had just finished eating a mercury-infused tuna sandwich after going for a three mile run. Learning to rely on medically induced cycles had kept me from distinguishing between actual pregnancy symptoms and hormonal side effects. After years of supporting each other, it wasn't surprising that I knew her cycle better than my own. Weird, yes, surprising, no.

This sudden omission of privacy isn't just associated with females. A male friend shared a rather intimate story about his fertility follies with his wife. After a particularly grueling talk on infertility, we somehow landed on the topic of the extreme measures that people take to ensure sex while ovulating. We never even remotely touched on this subject area before, and suddenly he was throwing it all on the table. During one of his wife's ovulation cycles she was out of town working at a youth ministry retreat. The site was about four hours away, but she was already a month or two into a heavy cycle of Clomid and they couldn't let a little thing like logistics get in the way of ovulation. They agreed to meet halfway to make the travel time fair, but while planning, didn't realize this was going to land them smack in the middle of the desert. Forget a hotel, the only thing around was cactus and waves and waves of scalding pavement. So, they practiced what teenagers have been perfecting for years, and attempted to procreate in their van. Just to be clear, this was the church van! Regardless of gender, everything is fair game when it comes to fighting infertility.

During this time Peter and I became friendly with a couple, Scott and Laura, who had also dealt with infertility. They recently had their first child and after some initial reluctance on my part, we made plans to meet for dinner. Since they fell into my accepted parental category of people who had experienced conception issues, I forced myself to temporarily step away from my baby quarantine. It is hard to stay bitter when looking at the innocent face of a newborn, and I was surprised to find myself enjoying the evening. Seeing the reward of someone who had tried so hard to have a baby, made my own chance at conceiving seem possible. I could feel my wall of resentment slowly chipping away as I relished in their new-parent happiness.

As the night was coming to a close, they handed me a gift. It was a simple handmade bracelet that spelled out the letters HOPE. Laura used to wear the bracelet for inspiration and as a reminder not to give up. They thought the bracelet could do the same for me. I was struck by their kindness and felt foolish thinking back on my initial hesitation towards seeing them. I began to wear the bracelet to my numerous office visits and tests. It would help to look at the letters and think of my friends and their newborn daughter. I now had something to remind me to keep hoping and the best part is that I even got to hold her.

A few years later on a trip with my son to visit family, I ran into a childhood friend. He introduced me to his wife, and I learned that they were dealing with fertility struggles of their own. I had never met her before, but there was an instant kinship. As she gazed at my newborn son, I couldn't help but recognize the sadness and longing in her face. Having my son had freed me from that desperation, but one look at her and I remembered it all. On my drive back home I couldn't stop thinking about her and what she was going through. As much as the bracelet meant to me, I knew what it could do for her. Honoring the kindness and tradition originally bestowed upon me, I packed up the bracelet and sent it her way. I heard from that same childhood friend recently, he told me after years of trying, his wife is pregnant and due this spring. Out of all the fertility treatments available, I think the kindness of others works best. Someday all will be fair in love and fertility, you just have to remember to hope.

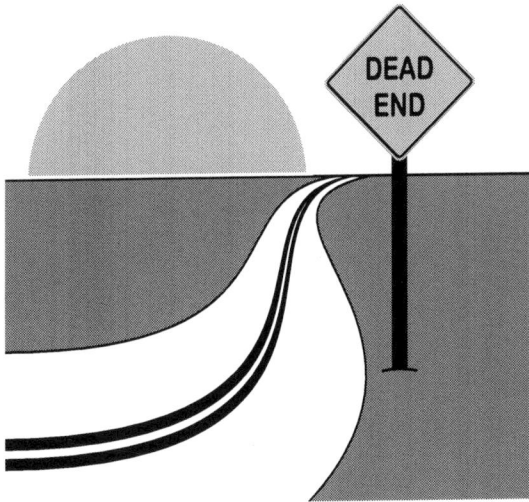

Chapter ⑥

The End of the Road –
In Vitro Fertilization (IVF)

The road from IUI to IVF (In Vitro Fertilization) is like driving along and hitting a dead end. When you're cruising along the hormonal highway it's a relatively easy ride. There may be detours along the way, but there are many routes to get you where you need to go. Clomid's not working? I'll take the exit for Follistim injections please. With IVF you are literally and figuratively at the end of the road. It's now or never and IVF is your last chance at giving birth to a genetic child of your own. The pressure mounts and you realize that IVF not only stands for your next procedure, but for your current status of I'm Very Fucked.

The decision to try IVF wasn't easy. All along the emotional rollercoaster of infertility, I never thought I'd get to this point. Being 32 and relatively young for an infertility client, I assumed I'd be an easy fix, a dream patient. I exercised regularly, didn't smoke, and came from a good old fashioned Irish brood. My sister was one of the .1 percent of people to actually get pregnant on the pill, and one of my brothers had five kids, including a set of twins. I was destined for baby making! I could get pregnant but I just couldn't stay that way, so why did I need help to get me to a place that obviously wasn't working? I was supposed to be a success story, not an IVF candidate.

The decision came by way of my fourth miscarriage. I had gotten pregnant on my last IUI attempt only to have it fail within the first few weeks. I was frustrated that despite everything I had endured, I was still unable to retain a healthy pregnancy. My doctor suggested we consider IVF. The rationale was that by hyperstimulating my ovaries, we would have more follicles to choose from. We would be able to hand pick the healthiest eggs for fertilization, thus reducing my chances for miscarriage. Scientific survival of the fittest, with my specialist playing the role of Darwin. A major downside was that as with all fertility treatments, there were no guarantees, and the financial stakes at this point were significantly higher. IVF was going to cost on average about fifteen thousand dollars and seeing the number on paper was staggering. Even though we had spent close to that amount on treatments over the years, it didn't hurt as much being spread out in smaller increments. IVF would require a huge leap of faith and unfortunately our resolve, as well as our bank account, was rapidly draining.

Each week meant another visit to the specialist's office and it was starting to take its toll. Peter and I were worn out mentally and physically, but couldn't fathom the idea of not having children. The one high note of the appointments was the clinic's close proximity to the beach. When my doctor advised IVF, we decided to go for a walk and digest the latest information. As we strolled along the sand, we debated whether to move forward with our doctor's recommendation. IVF was as risky emotionally as it was financially. Was it worth it to spend so much money, when there was the very real possibility of having nothing to show for it? Could I physically handle such an invasive treatment? My previous experience with a few added hormones would seem minimal in relation to the scheduled precision of IVF. My cycle would be directed by my doctor based on my ovaries producing the appropriate amount of eggs. If the fertility drugs worked their magic, my ovaries could be home to as many as 20 additional eggs at a time. Compared to the average of one per month, my body was sure to feel the effects. Pair this with minor surgery and daily injections, and the process was becoming as much of a deterrent as the high cost. Should I give up? Would I even be able to recognize when it was time to stop, or would I be stuck in this relentless cycle forever?

Every time I considered giving up, my nagging, almost obsessive, desire to be a mom would compel me to keep moving forward. It sounds simple, but as with most things in life, it's not. My husband and I had a great life. I married a warm, funny man who made me smile on the inside and out every day. I knew that if our life was destined to be just the two of us, I was luckier than most. When I was 13 my Mom passed away unexpectedly and abruptly. It was shocking and devastating and changed my life in more ways than I can describe. Growing up, I would watch my friends with their mothers and long for a connection like theirs. Although the stinging of my loss slowly ebbed away over the years, the desire for a maternal relationship did not. Realistic or not, having a child of my own would allow me a chance to get back a part of me that was irretrievably broken. Being a mother would help me to heal in a way that time would never offer. I could experience my own mother by becoming one. The thought that I might be cheated out on motherhood not once, but twice, felt sadistically unfair and drove me to continue on with years of fertility treatments. I would never forgive myself if I didn't wholeheartedly try, and I would forever be stuck with that ache in my heart.

Adoption loomed in our minds and I thought of the bond I could share with motherless children. I understood that need for family, and had a strong desire to fix these kids while fixing myself along the way. Peter and I both expressed feeling foolish spending such an exorbitant amount of money when there were plenty of children out there with kindness and love being the only kind of treatment required.

As we continued our walk we were no further along in our decision than before. We knew we wanted a baby, but just couldn't decide how. Should we stop treatment and move on to adoption, or would we be forever haunted by not trying every option available? I was overwhelmed and as with so many other times in my life, I wished my mom was there to help me. I needed someone, anyone, to make this decision for me. It was too hard, too raw, and I was at the point of breaking. I needed something to lead me in the right direction.

The sun was hot and we decided to take a break so we headed over to one of our favorite outdoor cafés. We had frequented this place more times that I could count, and loved its casual self-serve ambiance. The customers wait in line for a chance at placing their order, and are given a small placard to identify their meal to the servers. I selected a table and waited for Peter to return. When he sat down he had a funny look on his face. I couldn't place the look of confusion and asked him what was wrong. He tentatively showed me the placard we were given. On it was a picture of a bright, smiling, chubby baby. He had almost asked to replace it for fear of upsetting me, but it was so coincidental that he had to keep it. Looking around the café the other tables were dotted with images of trees, birds and even a bright big sunflower. In all the years we had been carelessly enjoying their Vermonster sandwiches and banana smoothies, this had never happened before. We were the only one with an actual human image, let alone that of a baby.

A few minutes later a small group pushing a stroller walked in and sat down beside us. The tables are so close it makes contact virtually impossible to avoid. Right away the baby took a liking to Peter and began to babble away in his direction. After some smiles and hello's we turned back to our lunch. A few bites later we were interrupted once again as the baby began to clamor for Peter's attention. When he finally looked over the baby smiled and as clear as day said, "Dada." Stunned, we couldn't help but look at each other and laugh. I'd spent the morning looking for answers and silently hoping for some sort of hidden guidance. The problem was I couldn't decipher the signs. Was this overwhelming baby presence something telling me not to give up? Should I go ahead with IVF or was the random baby calling Peter, Dad, a sign we should adopt? I was more confused than ever.

We went home and decided to think it over for a few days. No matter how we looked at the situation, it always involved the money. Even though money wasn't a driving force in our lives, we both recognized the significance of spending so much on something that wasn't even certain to get us any closer to our dream of being parents. Yet, weighing the decision so heavily around finances felt selfish and almost dirty. Although we tried to think of many other reasons not to give IVF a try, money was truly the main factor. We asked ourselves, what were we going to remember in twenty years, the money or the fact that we didn't bother to try?

With our proverbial thumbs out, we decided to take our chances on the open road. Whether we had an IVF baby or not, we knew we had to drive down every street before coming to that dead end. We took a deep breath, gave in and buckled up. Once again, we were headed down the hormonal highway and we were going to enjoy the ride.

Chapter **7**

The Male Perspective—
It's 98° Out Here!

The first time I recognized a difference in the way males and females dealt with infertility was when I found out I was pregnant with my son. After so many years of trying, I had finally made it to the elusive twelfth week. For a person with my history of four miscarriages without any live births in between, the rate of pregnancy success hung dismally between 0 and 5 percent. With a statistic like this any pregnancy, let alone a viable one, was a miracle.

Throughout my first trimester, I had weekly appointments with my specialist to ensure that the baby was still healthy and growing. The visits were met with competing amounts of happiness and despair. Despite having the security of a weekly checkup, the appointments were also an unavoidable reminder of the past. I had been in this position so many times before and the failed pregnancies always hovered close behind. It was a daily struggle learning to trust that this pregnancy might be different.

The weekly ritual of climbing onto the stiff examination table and waiting for the ultrasound to begin never got any easier. What were mere minutes would drag on, as I'd stare nervously at the doctor, waiting for any kind of reaction. Finally the screen would be filled with the flicker of the baby's heartbeat and I could breathe. The repetitive thump thump was undeniable proof of the baby growing inside me and with it came a glimmer of hope that this time I might really make it all the way to the end.

My baby high would be short lived. No sooner than leaving the doctor's office and the security of the ultrasound monitor, would doubt creep back in. Regardless of what I had seen a few minutes before, all of the previous miscarriages loomed heavily in the back of my mind. I knew that after coming this far and secretly allowing myself to believe that this time was going to be different, I'd be at great risk if the pregnancy failed. When the doctor finally confirmed that yes, we really were going to have a baby I couldn't believe it. I had harbored a great amount of skepticism that we'd actually make it through the first trimester. After all of the years of waiting, I was thrilled to finally be in the position to share some good news. I immediately thought of my dad, and bubbling with excitement, he was the first person I called.

My father raised me as a single parent from the age of 12, so even though he was a male he was often cast into many of the stereotypical female roles. He had to be content with pulling double duty and filling in for my mom on more than one occasion. He is a man of few words and his way of acknowledging that you did a good job is to tell someone else about it. He is the first to sing your praises, but never to you directly. Tell him you love him and he replies uncomfortably with, "Thank you." Living his life as a gruff commercial fisherman, he appears to be more at ease on the water, and raising children on his own couldn't have been something he anticipated. But despite his hard exterior he has a kind heart, and my siblings and I are truly loved. I thought nothing of including him in the wonderful news about my expanding family, and assumed he'd be as thrilled as I was.

This is when the big difference between males and females and their response to infertility came into play. I couldn't wait to share my news and I dreamily anticipated some sort of Hallmark-ish moment. Possible tears, joy, happiness, maybe even something akin to, "I knew you could do it and you'll be a wonderful mother." Something, anything, but what I got was, "Oh really? Hmm, uh, hmm. Did you know its 98 degrees out here?!" I couldn't believe my ears. Did he really just tell me how hot it was? Did he not hear me? I said it again and clear as day he resumed talking about the weather. Instead of parental words of wisdom, I had my own personal barometer. In utter disbelief I cried, "What? Are you kidding me? Do you know what I went through, how important this is, what this means to me? How long we have been trying?" The tears worked and I got a belated, "That's great news honey, wonderful, I have to go now." I hung up in shock and proceeded to stew.

It took me a few days to process his infatuation with comparing climates, but suddenly it dawned on me that no father, regardless of how evolved, wants to hear about his daughter's many attempts at making a baby. It goes against the core belief of parents. Children will never grow up and do the bad things you did, and more importantly, daughters will remain virgins forever, even after marriage. I think down deep my dad still saw me as the Virgin Mary. Sadly, the only Mary I could claim being a part of involved some vodka and a splash of tomato juice.

There were many times throughout my life that I longed for my mother. Times such as these were an unwelcome reminder that I was cheated by losing her at such a young age. Whether he liked it or not, I would often place my dad into a maternal role. Obviously from his weather comment he was much more suited as a father, but as a single parent he was forced to do both. Obviously from his weather comment, he was much more suited as my father, but he still attempted in his own way to do both. Not being one to let things go, I called him a few days later and apologized. I told him I realized discussing my pregnancy might make him uncomfortable, but this was something a mother and daughter would discuss, and like it or not, he was both. I promised to be sensitive to what I told him in the future, and by all means I did not expect him to be there for the delivery. He didn't provide me with an up-to-the minute forecast so I considered the conversation a success.

The difference between males and females surfaced again in the way my husband and I internalized our infertility. I don't think I fully understood or appreciated what he went through until years after we had our first baby. Although infertility affected both of us, I always felt it was harder for me because it directly involved my body. A friend we hadn't seen for a while asked about the results of our fertility tests. I told her we'd undergone a complete work-up and there weren't any concrete results. Peter's levels were fine, so the miscarriages were a mystery, that wonderful 33 percent in the unexplained category. She responded with, "So, the problem is all you then?" Without meaning to, her simple statement validated what I had been thinking for years.

Knowing that I was the one who was broken, I carried the burden and subsequent guilt with me at all times. No matter how kind or supportive Peter was, I still felt that he had to hold some resentment underneath. How could he avoid it when there wasn't anything wrong with him? He could have what we wanted most by finding a new partner, someone without all of the headache and probably longer legs and better hair. He could find a dream girl who wasn't an emotional wreck, someone more like the old me, smiling, fun, and full of laughter. Even I was beginning to tire of this new me. How could Peter, after all of these years of disappointment not feel the same?

No matter how many times he reassured me that that having a baby didn't mean anything if it wasn't with me, I still couldn't bring myself to believe him. My body was our obstacle and since I felt it was entirely my fault, I couldn't comprehend that it affected Peter as much as me. In some weird way I was almost jealous of him, jealous of the fact that he didn't have to go through the numerous tests and procedures. I was always the one getting poked and prodded, knocked out, cramped up, and scarred emotionally and physically. I know if Peter could have traded places with me he would have, but the sentiment just wasn't enough. Nothing could compete with what I was putting myself through.

It took some time for me to realize that this experience wasn't just about me. Every time I screamed about an unequal share of responsibility for our fertility process, was another reminder to Peter of his inadequacies as to what he could do to fix it. I may have hated going to all the appointments and sitting through the procedures, but they allowed me the opportunity to take an active role in treating my infertility. I had a place to expend my energy and although often futile, I could at least feel as if I was doing something to help our situation. Peter had to be content with sitting by and feeling helpless and hoping that random dinners and gifts of jewelry could replace some of the anguish I was going through (Note to the men out there, jewelry does work really well). Don't get me wrong, I am still using my many pokes and prods as a viable argument for a vasectomy, but I am now able to see that no matter how loud you scream, no one wins when it comes to infertility. No partner feels it more or less, it's awful any way you look at it.

Our differences were noticeable again when it came to having sex while pregnant. During our first pregnancy, I was determined to keep our marriage intact. We had been lucky enough to have a rare, great relationship and I had heard stories about how having children could drastically change a marriage. I was determined not to let that happen to us. We'd always be the same, still us, just with these adorable little babies that never spit up and slept peacefully through the night.

We'd always be the same, still us, just with these adorable little babies that never spit up and slept peacefully through the night. During my second pregnancy, I had convinced Peter that although pregnant, we could still maintain a healthy sex life. When that pregnancy failed, Peter was convinced that he had caused my miscarriage. Despite innumerous reassurances from our doctor that it was indeed okay to have sex while pregnant, Peter still felt that he played some role in making us lose the baby. Just as he would reassure me that the miscarriages

51

weren't my fault, I tried to do the same with him to no avail. Pregnant sex although great for others, was off limits in our house from that point on.

Years later after I had my son, we decided to try for another baby and were delighted that after only three months of trying I was pregnant. So it came as a big surprise when Peter looked at me sheepishly one day and said that he was more than grateful it wasn't going to take us another three years, but he really could have used another month or two of trying. I knew then that we had turned a corner. We were happy, safe, secure parents to be. But what was it that he was really saying? Was he suggesting that we actually have sex while I was pregnant? I just looked back at him and said, "Hey Petie, did you know it is 98 degrees outside?"

Chapter **8**

Jealousy,
The Green Eyed Monster

I finally got pregnant due to jealousy. Not IVF, not IUI, not having sex on a full moon with the bed facing east, or any of the other supposedly surefire ways to help get you pregnant. Don't get me wrong, I tried all of those methods and more. After four miscarriages, multiple failed attempts at IUI, and enough synthetic hormones to qualify for a change in sex status on my driver's license, I decided to give IVF a try. Never knowing that all it would take was a visit from the Green Eyed Monster to make all my problems go away.

With IVF (In-Vitro Fertilization), the process involves pumping your body full of hormones to hyperstimulate your ovaries so they can produce multiple eggs. When your body has reached a sufficient level, the eggs are then surgically retrieved, fertilized in a Petri dish with sperm, and transferred back to the uterus with the hopes that the eggs will continue to grow and develop into a fetus. When talking with others about their experience with IVF, everyone seems relaxed and excited. It's as if people are rolling off on their gurney to get a pedicure, not an anesthetized surgery.

I am the first to point out that I am a medical wimp. To this day, I still sweat before every checkup and no matter how many cookies they offer, I could never donate blood. I was terrified of undergoing IVF. The possibility of a baby was the only thing that kept me from running as far away from anyone in a white coat as possible. My fears were placated by the knowledge that after IVF there would be no more surgeries, no more hormones, and if I was lucky, no more tears and frustration. This procedure was our last chance and I could only close my eyes and hope that it would all be worth it.

The surgery wasn't as bad as I'd anticipated and knowing the hardest part was over, I began to feel some of the excitement I'd seen in others. I knew that as I sat and recovered, my eggs were hopefully multiplying, dividing and getting ready to be transferred back into my uterus in the days to come. Unfortunately, these feelings were short lived. I had a post surgery consultation with my doctor where he revealed that my eggs were genetically damaged. He gave me about a 5% chance of ever having a successful pregnancy. I was 33 years old and full of rotten eggs.

Despite the devastating news there was some comfort in knowing that we had finally found the reason behind all my miscarriages. Even with my untrained eye, the eggs on the specimen slides didn't look quite right. Instead of smooth perfect circles ripe for multiplying, mine looked like this process was making me, rough and wrinkled around the edges. Tiny sand-like granules spread throughout the specimen, creating a murky texture. We had three potentially viable embryos and even though it was highly unlikely a pregnancy would take, a slim chance was still a chance. Since we'd already come this far, the doctor said we might as well finish the procedure. With a heavy heart I agreed to schedule the transfer for the following morning.

That evening I finally broke down. My body was reacting to the stress of the past three years and I spent the night on the bathroom floor alternating between vomiting and crying. Forever in denial, my body was screaming out in a way that my mind wouldn't allow. I'd spent years convincing myself that everything would work out. Hearing the doctor's diagnosis put an end to any previous illusions I had for a happy ending. IVF was my last option, and discovering a genetic disorder was not the kind of result I was hoping for. Heading into the doctor's office for the transfer the following morning was about as close to hitting fertility rock bottom as I could fathom.

We implanted the embryos and left feeling discouraged and exhausted. I spent the next week trying not to think of the inevitable. I got my period about an hour after the doctor's office confirmed that none of the embryos had taken. The finality of the phone call and my body's monthly reminder to what we couldn't have was taking its toll.

At my next appointment the doctor reaffirmed that we were dealing with a genetic abnormality and there was nothing available to treat this. He suggested we try one of two options, get donor eggs or adopt. Donor eggs would allow us the opportunity to experience a pregnancy first hand by pairing my husband's sperm with that of an anonymous egg donor. Biologically, the child would be my husband's, but legally and in every other aspect, I would be the mother. The process would be the same as IVF except that instead of transferring my eggs, we would use those of the donor, which would finally enable me to undergo a full term pregnancy.

Cost was a significant factor. Donor eggs typically start at $10,000 and can range higher based on factors such as previous pregnancy success and the donor's educational background. The intended parents are also responsible for all medical expenses related to the procedure, including those of the donor. Bare minimum, this is at least $20,000 with no guarantees. I still had one round of IVF leftover from my original package. My doctor informed me that I could apply it towards the donor cycle, making us only additionally financially responsible for the donor's personal and medical fees. This would save a significant amount of money and keep my last IVF cycle from going to waste.

My husband and I sat and listened as the doctor described the egg donor process in detail. There was no denying the excitement that was unwittingly written on Peter's face when he realized the dream of having a genetic child of his own was not completely lost. I felt sick and riddled with guilt that once again it came down to me, self perceived or not, I was the problem. Even if for my sake Peter agreed to adoption, I would forever be haunted by my decision when the look on his face clearly stated the truth of what he really wanted. We got a referral for a donor agency and left.

Finding an egg donor is like going to Match.com for the infertile. There are hundreds of private companies with online databases full of potential donors. After providing some basic information you are given a password that enables you to look at individual profiles. Included are photos, details about their interests, and medical and educational backgrounds. On the rare time we did visit an actual agency, we browsed through a sampling of donors in a catalog. One woman stood out as a possible candidate, and before we knew it the agency was calling to check her availability. I sat there in stunned silence thinking that on the other end of the phone could be the mother of my child. If anyone else found this experience as strange as I did, no one said a word.

I have often said the only time my husband ever cheated on me was with a cup. During our search for the perfect donor there wasn't any cheating, but there was plenty of flirtation. We began to spend our nights sitting side by side viewing online profiles. Peter would be struck by a particular person and would excitedly ask, "What about her?" or point out, "She looks kind of like you." He was filled with the excitement that a new treatment could offer, but I was feeling increasingly left out. I always found something wrong with each person and wasn't thrilled to have a front row seat to the selection of my replacement. Instead of focusing on the positive, I began to find myself becoming irrationally jealous. If I couldn't even look at these women on a computer screen how was I going to embrace a child of theirs? I was jealous of the fact that they could offer my husband something that as a wife and a woman was my innate right. I was angry at these women, angry at my husband for seeming to enjoy the process too much, and most of all, angry at myself for putting us in this situation.

Despite innumerous reassurances from Peter, I couldn't push these feelings aside. I was depressed and feeling useless. I decided to take a weekend away to clear my mind. Denial had always been a friend to me and I was eager to escape. Peter and I had kept most of our feelings to ourselves, but it was common knowledge amongst friends that we had been trying unsuccessfully for years to have a baby. My weekend of dodging reality consisted of a few lazy days with some close friends at the beach. The talk inevitably came to the status of my fertility trials. When I relayed the latest in our follies, my friend, Danielle, casually said, "Why don't you just use one of my eggs?" I laughed it off and she persisted. We ended up discussing it in detail over the weekend and all of a sudden it didn't seem to be such a bad idea. Could I really pass her child off as my own? Our hair and eye colors were the same, and in fact many years earlier after I turned 21, I had given her my fake ID. If we could both pass for the same falsified version of Amanda Marie Cruz, then maybe, just maybe, this could work.

When I called Peter to tell him what was transpiring, he reacted with, "Danielle? She's hot. Sure we'll take her eggs!" Not amazement over the gesture (although that would be forthcoming), not relief at the possibility of not having to spend another $10,000, just she's hot. Peter's right, Danielle is hot and smart and incredibly kind, and all of the other attributes that you would hope your child to have. He did clarify that he was just excited to think how cute the baby would be, but irrational jealousy over some woman you will never meet is nothing in comparison with knowing that your husband thinks one of your close friends is hot.

We spent the next month seriously considering using one of Danielle's eggs, but somewhere along the way life sank in. This was so much more than helping out a friend in need, this would be her genetic child. How would I ever learn to explain to my child that Auntie Danielle was really their biological mother? Would Danielle want visitation rights or expect to be involved more than on a surface level? There were so many other layers to her offer and I just didn't know if either of us could handle it. I treasured our friendship and didn't want anything to ruin it. As selfless as her offer was, we had to decline.

Peter and I went back to surfing the donor sites. A few weeks into the search I found myself unable to continue. The stress of going through such heavy discussions with Danielle brought so many unresolved feelings to the surface that I had to stop. I couldn't bring myself to move forward with the donor process. I had been trudging along on autopilot and wasn't making informed decisions. With fertility treatments you are always watching some metaphorical clock. As if your biological clock isn't enough, you become obsessed with tracking the time up to ovulation, the time until you can test for pregnancy and, with each failure, the time until you can try again. It's a never ending cycle.

Each month begins with the hope that this time will be different and any break in treatment is an opportunity lost. Willingly stopping is acknowledging that you are going to let go. Even if only for a moment, it is terrifying. I knew I needed a break and despite a few lost chances at conception, what could a month or two hurt? Something inside was leading me further and further away from the donor process.

Crazy as it sounds, during my break I came to the realization that I wanted to give IVF another try. Even though I knew what my chances were, I felt compelled to do it again. Getting the same outcome would be the undeniable proof I needed to believe this genetic abnormality wasn't just a fluke. In order for me to accept an alternative form of parenting, I needed to be able to fully welcome a child without any questions or second guessing about the past. As practical as it was to use that last round of IVF for a donor cycle, I couldn't let money be the deciding factor. We had already spent so much money, more than I'd ever imagined possible, that what would it really save in the long run? My sanity was worth more than that. I told my doctor of my decision and we scheduled my IVF for the end of summer.

I had been pairing my fertility treatments with acupuncture and ever since my first session when I almost peed myself on her table, I had formed a trusted bond with my therapist, Jeneanne. Always hopeful and positive, she couldn't envision us giving up quite yet, so she did some research on genetic abnormalities and prescribed a few herbs and antioxidants. She also encouraged my return to an occasional glass of red wine and running. Both things I loved but, was advised to give up throughout my fertility trials. With nothing to take but vitamins, I decided to enjoy my first hormone free summer in years.

All of the missed opportunities and living life based on a fertility cycle had started to wear Peter and me down. As much as the summer was a break from the past, it was also a return to a life we had left behind. More than anything I wanted to enjoy this time with Peter and prove to him that I was worth keeping. Never had Peter made me feel as if he'd rather be with someone else, but I couldn't stop the envy from creeping back into our lives. Why was I like this? I was jealous over a connection I had been creating in my mind that my husband was going to have with some woman that he would never even have to meet. Irrational or not, this other woman would be giving him something that I couldn't, and it was eating me up inside. I couldn't help but wonder, was I no longer a complete woman in his eyes?

These thoughts were lurking in the back of my mind when we went out one night for some Mexican food and margaritas. Maybe it was the tequila, maybe it was the freedom to just be ourselves, but whatever it was I had to prove to the both of us that even though I was broken, I was still worth keeping. I had an illogical fear that I was at risk of losing Peter and the jealousy I felt towards these unknown women spurned me into action. I had to know that if our life was going to just be the two of us, we would be fine. I didn't want to be thought of as damaged goods, just as his wife and the one he loved and desired. Back was my confidence and my reminder as to what it was like to enjoy my husband. The threat of the other women slowly disappeared as Peter and I returned to our old life and each other.

A few weeks later I was shocked when I realized I was pregnant. What was I going to tell my doctor, that like some hormonal teenager I'd let my libido get the best of me and I'd actually had sex with my husband? Real sex, not doctor prescribed sex with a test tube or syringe or any other technological means of reproduction, just sex. Peter and I had spent so many years focusing on reproduction that we forgot all about its distant cousin, contraception. I was embarrassed that I'd have to explain to my doctor that we would need to adjust my treatment plan because sadly, I was convinced that this pregnancy, like all of the others, was going to end in miscarriage. I automatically calculated how long it would take for me to heal and get back on schedule for my last round of IVF so I could be pregnant again. Here I was hoping to miscarry one pregnancy so I could begin preparations for another. I was so jaded by the years of failed attempts that I couldn't even see the irony of my thoughts.

I truly believe that the kindness of others is the best fertility drug of all. Although I didn't end up using Danielle's eggs, her gesture and what it prompted me to do will never be forgotten. In some way, she did help me get pregnant. Without her offer I don't think I would have had the strength to slow down and take a break. That break led to not one, but two kids, and I will always be grateful for that. Whether it was the herbs and antioxidants, or just plain old jealousy, I'll never know. I think the Green Eyed Monster gets a bad rap, but like everything else, when channeled in the right direction he can be very useful. Well, that and a little dose of tequila doesn't hurt either.

Chapter 9

Miscarriage Miscommunication and I Miss You

I find it interesting that the word miscarriage begins with miss. If you look miss up in the dictionary you are given a wide range of definitions; to discover or feel the absence of, to fail to comprehend, and to escape or avoid. Grammatical coincidence or not, this is exactly how I coped with each of my miscarriages.

Although it is relatively easy to describe the physical aspects of a miscarriage, I find it virtually impossible to explain the emotional. How do you paint an adequate picture of something that changes on a daily basis? The emotional highs and lows of infertility can damage even the most positive psyche. Each treatment brings new possibilities and if they fail, whatever emotional armor you created, comes crashing down. One has to learn to successfully navigate through the upheaval that goes hand-in-hand with infertility. Anniversaries of past pregnancies, potential due dates, old sonogram pictures, even the baby section at the local department store, all have the potential to trigger an impromptu emotional breakdown. You can go from being a pillar of strength and optimism, to a crumbled pile of despair at the mere mention of another's pregnancy.

With each miscarriage it became that much more difficult to feign joy at other people's news. I found being around pregnant people only served as a cruel reminder to what I'd lost and was still desperately trying to find. It seemed as if everyone was pregnant but me. Babies and bellies were everywhere I went. Starring in my own personal horror show, I was unable to escape the sudden barrage of pink and blue. As the shower invitations piled up, so did my resentments. I found it increasingly difficult to celebrate other people's pregnancies when I was stumbling so badly though my own. Pregnant people forced me to deal with the reality of my situation and the possibility that I might never give birth to a child of my own. I had friends who were well into their second pregnancies before I'd even made it safely through a trimester. I was being obstetrically lapped and couldn't even get in the race.

To handle recurrent miscarriages, you have to be a glutton for punishment and have the ability to survive on nothing more than blind faith to willingly put yourself through pregnancy after pregnancy. There is no guarantee that the next time will end up any differently than the last, and the lack of security breeds a sense of paranoia. You can't help but convince yourself that it must be something you did, or even worse, didn't do. You didn't eat enough of the right foods or you had too much of the bad ones. You forgot to take that prenatal vitamin or the biggest oxymoron of all, you were stressed out. How is it possible not to become stressed when the key component of your treatment requires the daily monitoring of your body? It is ridiculous to assume that you can let go mentally when you are so physically involved. Your mind is constantly racing while it repeatedly challenges the undeniable proof of pregnancies past. The two events forge an unwelcome relationship and your confidence in successfully carrying a baby to term is stripped away with each pregnancy.

A miscarriage is greedy. It robs you of your child and takes away any remaining optimism for pregnancies to come. After so many disappointments, a positive pregnancy test came to represent everything except my belief at impending parenthood. With each miscarriage a pattern of sorts emerged. I'd get past the physical healing and move on to avoiding the emotional. My husband and I would try to convince ourselves that we would be fine living a life without children, and we'd appease ourselves by doing things that would be unreasonable for a new family. Visa sponsored vacations and manic shopping sprees were as much a part of my infertility tab as my IVF. I traveled a lot in those years and in each of my photos there is a silent image. Alongside us at the Grand Canyon is my first miscarriage, the vast emptiness of the landscape foreshadowing the years ahead. My third miscarriage smiles at me as I sit at the Farmers Market in Seattle, and the memory of the first time I sweated with fear as I injected myself with hormones cruised along with me in the Caribbean. I have more than my fair share of high spiky heels that could never keep up with a toddler, and handbags with no chance of surviving the crumbs and crayons of childhood. All of these trips and purchases are unwanted souvenirs of infertility and its aftermath.

Our society is ill equipped at handling death and depression. We prefer happy smiling faces or an oral cure-all for what ails us. Grieving makes people uncomfortable and when it is for something that for all accounts and purposes isn't there, we have an even harder time comprehending it. How can someone be so depressed over something that they never truly had? Are a few weeks really enough time to get attached to something? With a miscarriage, you grieve not just for the pregnancy but for the life that was beginning to be built around it. Despite all that a miscarriage takes, those visions of first steps, first words, of becoming a family, are cruelly the only things it leaves behind.

These feelings of profound grief aren't exclusive to those who have suffered miscarriages, coping with infertility is equally damaging. Although there is not an isolated physical loss, there is still a similar grieving process for the life that infertility patients can't attain. After one of my miscarriages I had someone bitterly tell me, "At least you can get pregnant." In the mind warping game of infertility being pregnant, even if only briefly, is one step closer to the dream of being a parent and sadly something to be envied.

Broken down, a miscarriage is little more than one big miscommunication between what your heart wants and how your body responds. Miscommunications have a way of turning into big disasters. My miscarriages were a disaster on my body and a disaster on my life. My once peaceful existence was turned upside down with no means for manually setting it right. When you are spinning so out of control it is hard to imagine that others aren't falling with you. Day-to-day life becomes overshadowed by the incessant tracking of cycles, and anything not related to your fertility tends to become an insignificant factor in your life. Friendships, your employment, and even your relationship with your partner, are all at risk for being left behind in the destruction of infertility.

In college, I formed a close bond with a small group of women. Each vastly different, we made up a unique brand of friendship that has continued to this day. Miscarriages and miscommunication almost changed that. One of these women, Kelli, was newly engaged around the time of my disappearance into infertility. I was pregnant at her wedding and suffered my third miscarriage shortly thereafter. With her new marriage and my fertility obsession, our contact became less and less frequent. I was shocked when she called me to tell me she was pregnant. She said they hadn't been trying and she was already at the end of her first trimester.

After three miscarriages and racking up bills for treatment, the words we weren't even trying stung almost as much as a pregnancy loss. I had been living my life doing nothing but trying, and the unfairness of the circumstance weighed on me as we stumbled through our conversation. Although we both felt it, neither of us spoke of the uncomfortable exchange that occurred between us. I extended a weak offer of congratulations and could do nothing to stop the surge of bitterness running through me as I hung up the phone.

I felt sorry for myself and questioned why once again, it wasn't me. I was doing everything by the book, taking every pill, enduring every shot, and engaging in any scientific simulated form of intercourse they'd throw at me. I was by all accounts and purpose a lab whore and to make matters worse, I was the one doling out the cash. Kelli and I kept in scattered contact over the next few months. Our conversations typically centered on fertility drugs and pregnancy pains. Kelli appeared to be having a rough time adjusting to the limitations of pregnancy and I found it cruel and unusually insensitive that she chose to confide such details to me. I couldn't understand what would compel her to complain to me about not being able to enjoy the occasional cocktail or gaining the extra pound or two. I would give up anything, everything, to be where she was and a wedge was pushed that much farther into our relationship. I never voiced any of my concerns and instead chose to stew in frustration as to why someone who didn't seem to appreciate being pregnant had gotten it so easily.

Each month brought Kelli closer to having her baby, and the realization that I was further away from motherhood than ever. An actual baby was materializing in front of me and this forced me to look at how much time had been wasted, how many babies I should have had by now. Coupled with Kelli's apparent distaste at pregnancy, I couldn't take it anymore. My self-preservation for motherhood kicked in and pregnant friends were kicked out. I began to retreat from the friendship until our conversations became less and less frequent and morphed into an occasional email.

Years passed and my friends from college and I ended up with kids around the same time. We decided that as new moms we needed to take some time to rejuvenate and revisit what was so special to us in college. We booked a three-day cruise and for the first time in years, all of us were together again. I was nervous about how the weekend would go. Kelli and I had recently begun a tentative friendship, but there was emptiness to our communication, both of us hanging on to unspoken hostilities from the past. The weekend was great, most surprising was how much I enjoyed spending time with Kelli. Our friendship picked up where it had left off and I had a reminder as to what it was beyond Disco Night at La Salles that we had connected so well about before. I came home pleased with the weekend but most of all, pleased with our renewed friendship.

Although we had resumed our relationship, Kelli and I had never talked about the obvious gap during those few years. When I began to write this book, Kelli was one of my first supporters. This led to a discussion on what it was like for her as one of the non fertility challenged, to be around me. As obsessed as I was, I never thought about what it might be like for someone on the other side of the spectrum, being forced to tiptoe around my emotions. Talking with Kelli I was stunned to learn that she had in fact planned her pregnancy, and all of the complaints and negativity were nothing more than a conscious effort on her part to spare my feelings. She explained that she felt it would be easier for me if she downplayed her pregnancy. As hard as it was for me to hear about her pregnancy, it was just as hard for her not to be able to openly share this experience. For years it had been all about my infertility, and for once Kelli wanted it to be about her and something positive. My life was at a standstill, but I shouldn't have expected others to keep from moving on and building families of their own. Kelli had every right to be excited about having a baby and my success at having one shouldn't have been a prerequisite. I should have been able to be her friend and celebrate during this special time, but I just couldn't.

When I learned what had really transpired, I felt nothing but sadness. Sadness that I missed out on such a special time in a friend's life and sadness that I didn't see how I was hurting her too. It took us over five years to have this conversation. Kelli pointed out that if I didn't have kids, we probably never would have been friends again. Kids were what pushed us apart and surprisingly, what pushed us back together again. What is most perplexing is that we never talked about this. I almost lost a dear friend due to miscommunication. Why didn't I just tell her how I felt? Why didn't she? We were both lost in our separate worlds of resentment, unable to clearly see what the other was going through. Instead we chose to ignore what was painfully obvious and did nothing to stop the hurt from spreading even deeper into our relationship.

When dealing with infertility, it is normal to have feelings of jealousy and resentment. The tendency to isolate oneself from pregnant friends or those with small children can be expected. You have the right to remove yourself from situations that can be detrimental to your mental well being, but this right isn't a free pass. It is still important to communicate with others about what you are experiencing and why you may be pulling away. Discussing these feelings will help others understand what you are going through and open the door for additional support.

Real communication is difficult and risky, but friends are worth the risk. It may have taken five years, four miscarriages, and a lifetime worth of miscommunication, but all it took to get it back was a simple, "I miss you and I'm sorry." Thankfully, there's no miscommunicating that.

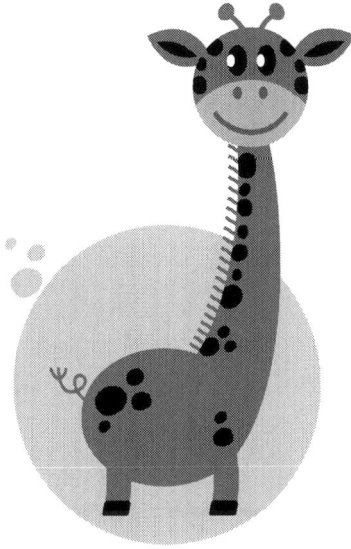

Chapter 10

Special Giraffe

Somewhere between hunting for donor eggs and jealousy, I almost gave up. After years of guesswork and empty results, the cause of my infertility had finally been diagnosed. A genetic disorder was the culprit behind my recurrent miscarriages, and a viable pregnancy was about as likely as a day without added hormones.

All it took was a brief 30-minute session in a sterile medical office, and my internal debate was finally over. I was never going to have a biological child of my own. It was an anticlimactic ending to years of treatment with nothing more than two little words. I was finally freed from the relentless guess work of infertility, but the cost of that freedom was more than I could bear. I'd dreamt of finding the reason for my miscarriages, never anticipating there wouldn't be a cure. Once again I was reminded that I truly had no control over my fertility. The doctor officially confirmed what I already knew, that I was as screwed up on the inside as I was on the out.

I sank into a quiet state of shock and depression. Despite the years of disappointments, there had always been other options available. Some new drug or procedure would anesthetize the pain and fuel my momentum for experimenting with further treatments. The diagnosis of a genetic disorder took all this away and effectively ended any naïve illusions that I was just one step away from maternal bliss. Our doctor's suggestion to adopt or use donor eggs provided us an opportunity to parent, but I was still getting used to the idea of it not being on my own terms, let alone in my uterus.

Our pity party was moving along at full swing, and being holed up in our house was only making it worse. In a moment of rare clarity, Peter and I decided to step away from the gloom and spend a day at the local Wild Animal Park. One of my favorite exhibits involved feeding giraffe's over a fence. For a few dollars you could purchase a sack of leaves that the giraffes would eagerly eat out of your hands. Their tongues were dark, almost black, and ridiculously long. It was impossible not to laugh as they used them to swirl and slobber the leaves down. It sounded like the perfect way to escape the cloud hanging over our heads.

On the way to the Wild Animal Park, you pass Orfila Vineyards. Back when we got married, Peter and I had selected the winery for our wedding site, and impulsively we decided to stop in. I obviously wasn't pregnant, nor was I about to be, so enjoying some wine and conversation seemed to be a good idea. The place was as beautiful as we remembered. Cool green grass surrounded the tasting room, and there were picnic benches and rose bushes scattered throughout. A terracotta fountain sits in the middle of an oversized tented area that we had used for our reception. As we walked around the site, memories of our wedding came flooding back. I could hear the clanking of glasses, the laughter of family and friends, and feel the happiness that comes with being young, in love, and worry free.

I thought of my dad's toast, Peter's smile, and the look of terror on the caterers face when our guests mistook our ceremonial smashing of Greek plates as an opportunity to do the same. Our life had always been blissful and easy. It was one of the things that attracted me to Peter the most, his natural ability to make me laugh and enjoy the simple act of living. Our years of dating had been relatively smooth. We navigated a long distance relationship early on, and after some initial shock over my penchant for too many house plants and Peter's love of quirky art, we seamlessly moved in together. Marriage came shortly thereafter.

Peter and I had never experienced a rough patch and at the time, it scared me. I was the first in my family to get married, coming from parents who divorced and a family with a preference for long term living arrangements versus traditional marital vows. Marriage was honored, but never pushed or required. I loved Peter and believed no better reason to get married than that, yet I was wary of the happiness around me. My biggest fear of getting married wasn't the commitment, it was the rain cloud that seemed destined to follow. Being newly engaged, people were eager to offer advice and we were plied with suggestions on navigating through the difficult times. It appeared that these moments of marital interruption were some sort of rite of passage required of all married couples. With our peaceful history, I worried if we'd be able to cope as well as a couple when challenged. I never anticipated this challenge to be infertility, and not our ability to continually love each other.

It dawned on me as we sat there with the ghosts of our wedding that this was what people were referring to. We were in the midst of one of those defining points in a marriage, a rough patch, even though it had nothing to do with us. Infertility had become our struggle, but we were surprisingly still the same. We wanted children and hoped creating a family would be a part of our life, yet sitting there being pulled back to where we had begun, I was reminded of what I had right in front of me. We didn't get married to have children, we got married because we liked each other. We had fun, we laughed, and this would continue with or without children. Regardless of how badly we wanted kids, I knew that Peter and I would be okay. It was liberating to let go of the pressure of creating a family and remember to enjoy the one I already had. Suddenly, the thought of not having children didn't seem as empty, and I was relieved to feel the panic of childless living slowly fade away.

The day escaped us and by the time we finally made it to the Wild Animal Park, they were closing. Peter managed to slip inside the gift shop and he returned with a simple present, a small plastic giraffe. Even though we never made it to the exhibit, the giraffes still worked their magic. Once home, I placed the giraffe on my bedside table as a reminder of what was truly important. Eventually, it fell into a drawer along with some old magazines where he stayed until my daughter dug him out a few years later. When she asked where he came from I said that he was Special Giraffe and that Daddy had given him to me to make me smile. He became one of her favorite playthings and thanks to many additional trips to the Wild Animal Park, he now has a family of his own. They all live happily in my daughter's room and there is nothing more special than that.

Chapter 11

Practical Advice from a Reformed Clomid Addict

I always adhered to the belief that drugs and pregnancy don't mix, right up until I had to develop an addiction in order to get pregnant. I find it strange that there is even such a thing as fertility drugs. Isn't it common knowledge the damage substances can have on your body, let alone a developing fetus? Yet, when dealing with infertility, people eagerly line up for the latest drug on the street. Our white coat pimp is paid top dollar to outsource us for sex, and any notions of maintaining intimacy are immediately replaced with scientific foreplay dictated by a plastic cup. From the ultrasound technician, to the highly recommended herbalist, everyone is a dealer and they all want their cut.

Before you know it, your casual usage becomes a full-fledged addiction and you find yourself selling your possessions for a round of IVF. That's how it was for me with Clomid, the hot flashes a mere penance for the chance to have a child. I was hooked, willing to do anything to recapture the elusive high that only a pregnancy could create. Having lost faith in my body's ability to create a child, I manically fixated on jumping from one failed treatment to another. My obsession momentarily eased by the array of options placed before me. A prescription for Clomid paved the way for an IUI, and the heroin of all fertility treatments, In Vitro Fertilization, was soon to follow.

Unlike their illegal counterparts, fertility drugs offer nothing to enhance your life. No purported euphoria or exaggerated confidence, just weight gain and mood swings that flirt dangerously close to insanity. I went from being a self described needle-phobe to a white collar junkie. I was a pro at injecting myself and although I still had my teeth, I only used them to growl at my husband through. My treatment plan had morphed into an addiction and I found myself saying yes to whatever the doctor ordered. The emotional wreckage of each failure was smoothed over by the calendar crack coveted by us fertility junkies. Nothing can appease you more than trying again, and the 7-14 day countdown to ovulation offers a high like no other. Anything is possible, even the belief that this will finally be the month you get pregnant.

Hitting rock bottom was triggered by Peter's online search for my uterine doppelganger. Under no circumstances was I comfortable with my husband looking for a replacement in that area. Scientific or not, I couldn't bear the thought of his admiration of another woman's nether regions. Despite the generosity of being entrusted with someone else's eggs, all I could think about was what these other women were giving Peter, blind to the gift being made available to me. Years of fixating on nothing but my infertility made me afraid to face the thought of my genetics not being a part of the solution. I couldn't handle any more uncertainty, and for the first time I thought about what was right for me and finally said no to a treatment.

Finding the strength to slow down and listen to my body was an integral point in learning how to cope with my infertility. When I realized I'd accidentally gotten pregnant, I never expected it to stick. I was so consumed with IVF being the miracle solution that I failed to hear what my body was trying to communicate on its own. As the weeks and my pregnancy progressed, I surprised myself by letting go. I gave up trying to control my fertility and let nature take its course. For once, nature was on my side, and I was happily able to move on.

As a recovering addict, I still wince when I see a set of stirrups and I suffer the occasional post-traumatic hot flash. Surviving infertility was one of the hardest things I ever had to overcome. It became impossible to imagine a life not tied to infertility and I seriously doubted if I would ever have a child. The support of others was crucial, and an invaluable component in helping me during this time. With this in mind, I've put together a list of survival tips for those currently wading through the hormones and hot flashes of infertility.

The **12** Step Program to Surviving Infertility

Step **1**

To Tell or Not To Tell? – Finding the balance between creating a support system and letting the mailman in on your sex life

One of the hardest parts of coping with infertility is the isolation that becomes such an integral part of the process. A question as basic as, "Do you have children?" can be unwittingly loaded with pain and emotion. You repeatedly find yourself in the uncomfortable position of determining how much to divulge and to whom.

With many cases of infertility spanning across years, dodging questions can become exhausting. Side effects from hormone treatments and an above average amount of doctor's appointments are hard to cover up. The loneliness that accompanies infertility can be diffused by sharing your experience with others, but how do you determine who to tell? When establishing a support system it is helpful to consider the following:

- Is this person is a close friend or casual acquaintance?
- Is this someone that you can rely on for emotional support?
- If you had a pregnancy or fertility treatment fail, how would you feel about this person knowing?
- Are they trustworthy enough to keep your details in confidence if asked?

With my second pregnancy, I prematurely told many people around me about my happy news. Considering most people move on to have healthy pregnancies after suffering a miscarriage, I never thought to wait until the end of the first trimester when most pregnancies are considered secure. This became instantly regrettable when I had to backtrack and inform people that I had lost the pregnancy. The painful exchange proved to be uncomfortable for me and most of those involved. Sharing with close friends and family is to be expected, but I overzealously told anyone who would listen. From this point on, I chose only to tell people who would be a direct source of support in the case of a miscarriage or failed treatment.

As hard as it can be to talk about infertility, sharing your experience is a great way to receive help during this time. According to The Center for Disease Control and Prevention, more than 7.3 million Americans, or 1 in 8 couples of childbearing age, are infertile. With statistics like that, it is likely to have affected someone you know. Other survivors of infertility can be a wonderful resource for providing coping techniques and emotional support. For a more structured or anonymous setting, consider joining a support group. RESOLVE (The National Infertility Association) and AFA (The American Fertility Association), both provide a wealth of online and group support options.

Step 2

Alternatives to hitting the person who tells you to *Just Relax* and other useless information

Throughout my years of infertility I was given many unsolicited words of advice, most of which was completely useless. Suggestions such as just relax or you just need a vacation, aren't meant to be hurtful, but they imply that you have some sort of control over your fertility. These comments can inadvertently come across as dismissive and minimize the devastation felt when one is unable to conceive.

Well meaning people will often begin a sentence with *did you*. Did you take all of your vitamins? Did you continue to exercise? Did you drink before you found out you were pregnant? Unintentionally there is a sense of blame put on the individual and this can be emotionally damaging. Although the comments come from a place of concern, it is hard not to negatively internalize them. Guilt is already such an integral part of the infertility process and these remarks help fuel your irrational fear that you must be doing something wrong. It is important to remember the basis of these statements comes from a place of concern, and people in general are trying to help.

A perfect example of this comes from my favorite piece of bad infertility advice. My brother, JP, is a father of five whose only experience with infertility is his inability not to impregnate someone. He had children with such ease that I threatened to Rumpelstiltskin him and claim the next one for myself. After one of my miscarriages he reminded me to stay positive, that the best part of babies was making them. I don't know what was worse, his advice or the fact that he was talking to me about sex. I highly doubt he was aware that by now all baby making included a third party, and not the kind that some would call fun. If the process of infertility hasn't drained all of the zest out of your relationship, the syringes and test tubes will surely do the trick. He meant to be helpful, but the implication that baby making should be looked at as fun isn't even a remote possibility for someone coping with infertility.

Unless directly affected by infertility, it is hard to comprehend how truly debilitating it can be. If possible, when you find yourself engaged in minimizing dialogue, talk to the person about why the remark can be perceived as hurtful. Explaining what you are feeling can initiate communication, and by educating them the person may become a means of support instead of added stress. My brother's advice wasn't ideal, but in his own way, he was trying to offer support. Instead of focusing entirely on the delivery, it helps to understand one's intention and accept the support. Communication will help bridge the gap between educating and supporting one another on this sensitive topic.

Step 3

Inquiring Minds Want to Know – How to handle probing questions

Questions about one's personal life are a normal means of communication. For someone in the midst of treatment for infertility, the answer isn't always clear. Once again you find yourself in the predicament of determining who to share intimate details with. It is reasonable to assume that in group settings questions of a more personal nature will be asked. Consider the type of questions that may arise, and have a variety of prepared responses on hand. In some cases, you may want to excuse yourself from social gatherings until you are emotionally ready to handle these types of interactions. It can be helpful to pair your response with a question to help steer the course of conversation. A reply such as, "I don't have kids at this time. Can you tell me what brings you to this dinner party/meeting/event?" should enable you to direct the conversation to that of a more neutral topic.

When dealing with a co-worker or acquaintance that you might see on a more regular basis you may need to be more direct to avoid the topic being brought up again in the future. "This is something of a personal nature and I'd rather not discuss." Or you may use the humorous approach and say, "Only my husband/wife/dog/etc., they keep me so busy I sure feel like I have kids."

There may be times when someone doesn't pick up on your social cues and honesty may be your only option. You should never be ashamed of what you are going through and if necessary, let someone know. "We're working on it" or "I hope to" might be enough to let someone figure out this is a sensitive subject. Using the direct approach of "We've been struggling to have a child and this is a personal matter that I'd rather not discuss" or "This isn't something I am comfortable discussing" both convey the message that this is a private, sensitive topic. Redirecting the conversation or excusing yourself can help keep these topics from resurfacing.

Step 4

Coping with a Miscarriage or Failed Treatment

Dealing with infertility requires an immeasurable amount of strength. The continual cycle of highs and lows can take a toll on one's emotional and physical well being. Coping with a miscarriage adds an extra component of fear to an already delicate state of mind. After a loss there is endless worry that each pregnancy will have the same result. With a miscarriage, you are forced to let go of your dream of being a parent and it is natural to become angry and depressed. The baby in your body was real, as was the life you were creating around it. It is important to take the time to allow yourself to heal and say goodbye to old dreams before you can make room for new ones.

Experiencing a failed fertility treatment can trigger similar feelings of loss. The preparation for assisted reproductive techniques is lengthy. With so much time and emotion built around one event, it is crushing when the procedure fails. All of your focus has been put towards this one event and it is a welcome distraction. If a treatment fails, the individuals involved have to cope with that loss and come to terms with not having the family they envisioned come to fruition. Just as with a miscarriage, you have to learn to manage these highs and lows, and cope with the debilitating process of determining whether you can emotionally and financially risk trying again.

To help cope during this emotional time, enlist a trusted friend to make calls on your behalf. Having to relive the nightmare of your miscarriage or share the disappointing news that a treatment didn't take, can be a heavy burden during such an emotional time. For those who offer to help, accept it, even if for something as simple as a meal. The kindness of others will lift your spirits and remind you of what you still have to be grateful for.

Without the presence of an actual child it is easy to try and dismiss the loss. Ignoring or repressing your feelings can cause undue stress when they eventually surface. It's critical to your well being to take care of yourself and return to treatment only when you feel it is right for you. It is a necessary and critical step in the healing process to move forward only when one is physically, as well as emotionally, ready.

Step 5

Holidays and Special Events –
When Mother's Day or baby showers become anything but celebrations

As much as you try, it is impossible to avoid some key trigger dates when dealing with infertility. Baby Showers, Mother's Day, and potential due dates can be some of the most difficult times to manage. There is no escaping these days and in many cases, the anticipation is worse than the reality. It is important to recognize your limits, and if necessary, excuse yourself from participating in baby centered events. Be honest with those involved about how difficult these situations can be, and try to honor them in a way that meets both of your needs. A lack of participation can be misconstrued if the individual is unaware of what you are going through. Taking care of yourself is imperative, but it is also important to consider the feelings of those around you. Maintaining communication with others will help ease the strain of personal relationships during this time.

With infertility, you spend so much time being angry about what your body doesn't do that it can be easy to forget to be thankful for the things it does. The multitude of drug therapies, procedures, and surgeries can take their toll on your physical well being. Use these emotionally charged days as an opportunity to enjoy what your body can do. Take a hike or a long walk, attend a yoga class or invigorate yourself with a run. Spend some time gardening or any activity that will get you moving and remind you to be thankful for the gifts that your body still provides. Taking the day and turning it into something positive can help ease the negative association often felt during these times.

Step 6

Even my Dog is Pregnant –
How to handle the baby boom around you

After four miscarriages and more fertility treatments than I can count, I would think I should be able to answer the age old question, "Is it just me or were there always this many pregnant people around me?" I had never seen so many pregnant people and babies before, but suddenly they were everywhere, like those Croc shoes that shouldn't be worn by anyone over the age of five. Watching everyone else multiply like rabbits can have a negative effect on your patience. I am ashamed to admit that during the latter part of my years with infertility, I took to avoiding anyone who was pregnant or had a new baby. I would convince myself that there was a reason why they didn't deserve a child as much as I did and this sanctimonious attitude gave me the permission I needed to hide.

Self preservation begs room for all kinds of behavior. I am not proud of how I acted, but I also understand that putting myself in family centered environments was doing more harm to me than good. Communicating why I was retreating from these relationships would have helped avoid countless amounts of unnecessary stress and conflict. If you suddenly find yourself in the predicament of being seated in between a pregnant lady and a newborn, it's simple, get up and move. Metaphorically or not, acknowledge that the current situation is not healthy for you and allow yourself the freedom to take a step back. Don't force yourself to do something for the sake of appearances. If that means temporarily skipping out on baby showers or spending less time with a close but expectant friend, give yourself the option to do so. Remember that despite what you are going through this is still a special time for those involved. Be honest about your situation and how you feel. Oftentimes just having the conversation is enough to get you past your emotions and give you the strength to continue the friendship.

As hard as it may be, try not to make assumptions. With such high rates of infertility, the person sitting next to you may have experienced difficulty themselves. Instead, use all of the pregnant people around you as a reminder to how many people have overcome infertility, and in time that person may very well be you.

Step 7

Navigating the Land of *If* – Putting your life on hold

I came up with a unique coping mechanism while dealing with infertility. I'd get invested in a new type of medication or treatment and I would be convinced that by this same time the following year, I would be pregnant. With 12 attempts laid out before me, my optimism would be at its peak. I'd appease myself with statistics and envision my future with the newborn

I was sure to have. As the months progressed and my chances were dwindling, I'd adjust my thinking to, "By this time next year I'll be six months pregnant." Or, "By this time next year I'll be finishing my first trimester." Living in the life of *What If* made the everyday monotony of infertility bearable, but created unavoidable reminders when those days came and passed, and I still wasn't any closer to having a baby than before.

I would avoid scheduling vacations or would be afraid to have a glass of wine all based on the elusive *what if?* While it is important to allow yourself to dream, you also need to be careful that it doesn't overshadow your reality. As much as possible, continue to live your life normally. Denying yourself things that make you happy will hurt that much more when the *what if* becomes *I'm not.*

If something makes you happy and is safe, go ahead and live your life. For our five-year wedding anniversary, my husband and I had planned a trip to Maui. Three other couples were also joining us. The trip was to be a last hurrah before attempting IVF again that fall. Shortly after booking our trip I found out I was pregnant again. Upon arrival, I would be about eight weeks along, typically the time when I would miscarry. If history were to repeat itself, there was a very good chance I would either be healing from or having a miscarriage on my vacation. Instead of cancelling the trip, we decided to go anyway. This being my fifth pregnancy I knew the drill and reasoned there wasn't a better place to have a miscarriage than

Maui. Why be laid up in bed at home when I could at least have an oceanfront view? The days that usually dragged by during the first trimester were sped up with the diversion of a vacation.

I felt safe floating in the water with friends and family close by. I gave in to the realization that I couldn't control what happened and stopped living by the code of *what if* and just lived. I made it through the vacation and more importantly, through the pregnancy. When faced with infertility it is inevitable that your life is going to change. There is no escaping the various treatments and procedures, but you can still have a life, just a slightly more puffed up version of your old one, but a great one none the less.

Step 8

It's Not Your Partners Fault They Aren't Getting Poked – Keeping your sanity and your relationship

In most cases of infertility, one person typically receives the brunt of testing and treatments. There is a physical inequity to the process that can easily be transferred into friction. Compounded with the sensitivity of the topic, there is a lot of stress generated during this time. Couples internalize their infertility in different ways so it is natural to be at different places emotionally throughout the process. One person may be ready to move forward to another form of treatment, while the other may still need time to comprehend the situation. By keeping the lines of communication open, this will help to alleviate some of the tension during this time.

Try to remember that you entered this process as a couple and although it may not always feel that way, it affects both of you equally. Date nights may sound like the beginning to an end, but scheduling time out for just the two of you will force contact and help keep the basis of your relationship in perspective. Set aside time for something not related to your issues with infertility. Go on a bike ride, take a tour of one of your town's tourist attractions, or visit places that are special to you as a couple. In addition to strengthening your relationship, you are also getting some valued time as a couple that won't be as easily available once you are a new parent.

Continued communication is extremely important. Talk about where you are emotionally with your treatment plan. Respect each other's need for processing each step, and honor where you are individually before moving on to the next step together.

Step 9

Smashing the Rose Colored Glasses – Dealing with the anger and frustration of infertility

My friend Val once told me I lived life as if walking around wearing rose colored glasses. I took pride in having a positive attitude and was shocked to watch it disappear along with each failed pregnancy. It is hard to stay optimistic when despite doing everything right, it still turns out wrong. The anger builds and chips away at the remaining optimism you have for creating a family.

Keeping your feelings pent up inside can be damaging to your mental health. Managing this stress will help combat some of the disappointment and encourage you to keep going. Channel your feelings and release this energy by smacking golf balls at a driving range, visit a batting cage, or take a kick boxing class. Running has always been my favorite escape and as my feet would pound into the pavement I'd slowly begin to feel more like myself. Find an activity that you enjoy and include it as part of your treatment plan. Complimenting rough days with a favorable activity will help relieve some of the anger you are struggling with.

Infertility takes so much from you and being angry is a normal, beneficial part of the process. It is liberating to let go of these feelings and move on in your treatment. Living your life wearing rose colored glasses is great, but accidents do happen. Inevitably the lens will get smashed, and you just have to learn to pick up the pieces and put on a new pair.

Step 10

Coping with Negative Thoughts

Negative thoughts can become overwhelming when struggling to have a family. Undergoing repeated treatments can lead to questioning and self doubt, and for those who have suffered a miscarriage, there is an additional element of fear that becomes linked to pregnancy. It is hard to dispute history and despite ones best effort, the past pregnancies are always lurking close behind.

Bouts of negativity and apprehension towards your ability to conceive are a natural part of dealing with infertility. Identifying these feelings and creating a set of coping mechanisms can help get you through these difficult periods. If you are fearful that you won't be able to get pregnant, reassure yourself with all that you are doing to help push the process along. Each test, poke and prod ultimately brings you that much closer to becoming a parent. These extra measures may not be wanted, but whatever child you end up with is a direct result of these current struggles. Acknowledge that you are doing everything you can and thank yourself for what you are doing to make this happen.

If you are pregnant, recognize when negative thoughts about miscarrying enter your mind. Establish a system to help draw you away from the negative thoughts. Write out any harmful thoughts, or say them aloud to your partner or a close friend. Talk about what you can do to keep these images from coming back into your mind. Be aware of triggers that get these thoughts in motion and redirect your thinking towards something positive. Learning to manage these thoughts will help allow you to focus on what is important, your goal of becoming a parent.

Step 11

Wading Through the Fads

It seems like there is always a magic new treatment when it comes to infertility. It wasn't until 1978 with the conception of Louise Joy Brown, the world's first successful test tube baby, when research for infertility truly began to take hold. Considering how relatively young this science is, it points towards a positive future for the treatment of infertility. But what does this mean for those who are struggling today? How can you tell the difference between potentially cutting edge technology and hype?

Never being able to determine the cause of my miscarriages, I spent a lot of time ruling things out. I felt as if I was playing some sort of medicinal game of bingo where exploratory surgeries and changes in prescriptions were all part of some elusive winning combination. As my options started to fade, an internal panic set off and I began looking closer at alternative methods of treatment. This quest was driven equally from frustration with my current lack of medical success and the realization that I was running out of things to try. This type of thinking can get very expensive. Your infertility tab is high enough and when you start to add additional services such as acupuncture, naturopathy, nutritional services, therapy, it all starts to add up. It is hard not to let the panic of infertility rule your choices as well as your bankbook.

To help match you with the right provider or alternative option, try the following:

- Ask around, word of mouth is the best form of a referral available. Find out what worked for other people who also dealt with infertility.
- Research the individual and ask for referrals. Check online to see what has been written about the type of service or the provider that you are looking into.
- Come prepared to your initial meeting with questions about what can be expected during the course of treatment, both physically as well as financially.
- Be wary of guaranteed success rates or higher than average percentages. In quoted studies, ask for the amount of participants involved. It is easy to have a high success rate if the control group is small.

- Go with what feels right for you. Infertility is a trying process, and it is important to be surrounded by people you trust, and who can help you along the way.
- Check with (ABORM) The American Board of Oriental Medicine or Acufiner.com for standard practices and professional referrals.

Being open to new experiences and treatments can help make the stress of infertility manageable. Take the time to find a complimentary treatment that feels right for you. If you feel uncomfortable doing something, walk away. These services are supposed to help support a potential pregnancy and it is important to put your personal needs first during this critical time.

Step 12

Throwing in the Gown – Knowing when to say when

Infertility has a way of taking over one's life. The constant physical tracking can begin to become nothing more than a painful reminder of what you fear you'll never be able to attain. If you find yourself at risk of running on autopilot, moving through the motions of treatment, give yourself the freedom to let go, even if it's only for a short while. Spend a day with a close friend who can help lift your spirits and make you laugh. Read a book, get a pedicure, or indulge in something decadent. Honor all that you do to make your dream of having a family come true. Spend some time doing nothing more than something that makes you happy.

Healing from the failure of a treatment or pregnancy is critical to your mental well being before moving on. If you find yourself unable to take the next step back towards treatment, seek out the advice of a trusted friend or professional. Be honest with your partner and doctor about what you are feeling. The path to parenthood is different for every person. Some people have the ability to cope with infertility for years, while others may decide the emotional risk is just too high. Whether you choose to continue with treatment, adoption, or maybe even childless living, that decision is personal and can only be made individually. These answers can be found by nurturing yourself and honoring what feels right. The first step in mothering is taking care of someone, even if that person is you.

I have now been a Mother longer than the time I struggled to become one. Sometimes it seems as if those dark years didn't really exist. My heart has healed and on occasion I even forget what it took to create my family. I recently cleaned out some drawers and found a journal dated back to my years of infertility. An entry was written to the child I was carrying at the time. My writings revealed that I was scared I would lose the pregnancy, but hopeful it would work. My last lines were wishing the baby a safe goodnight. That pregnancy was my third miscarriage.

Like any addiction, these demons lie quietly underneath, ready to appear when you least expect them. I became saddened for that baby and what Peter and I went through. I am able to find peace in knowing that those losses weren't in vain. Every failure brought me closer to my greatest success of all, my two children. I will never truly know why those early pregnancies didn't work, or what those children would have become. All I know is that I am grateful for the family that I have, and that is something I can surrender to.

Chapter 12

Full Circle

Her name was Julia and I met her at a women's retreat. She was fresh off her first miscarriage and the anger was still seeping out of her like a film. Bitterness was courting her on a daily basis as she tried desperately to make sense of her loss. We had a mutual friend who tried to connect us before. With my history of miscarriages she thought I might be able to help. Despite her intentions there wasn't anything I could do, and in reality, I would probably make things worse.

To someone new to infertility, I represented a worst case scenario, so much more than a simple case of bad luck. Although it helps to learn about someone successfully conceiving after a miscarriage, you don't want to believe it could take you years of treatment and multiple pregnancy losses to get there. I am the statistical outlier and proof that miscarriages do happen more than once. The only consolation of a miscarriage is realizing how common they are. On average, one in five pregnancies ends in miscarriage, and most people continue on to have healthy, normal pregnancies. This fact becomes your truth and the drive behind trying again. For someone trying to move past their loss, I may as well be the grim reaper of fertility come to take any remaining confidence for pregnancies to come. Instead of helping, I could do nothing but provide an increased sense of paranoia and fear. I wasn't surprised that I never heard from Julia.

At the retreat a group of us sat around a table casually discussing our lives. I was introduced as a writer and this led to a discussion about the topic of my book. There were multiple conversations going on at once, but when I began to speak one woman looked across the table and froze. I instantly knew from the look on her face that she had dealt with infertility. She seemed to want to ask questions but was hesitant, content for the moment with listening in. As the group dispersed, she lingered for a few moments before introducing herself as Julia. We spoke for a short while before she revealed that she'd recently had a miscarriage. She was searching for answers and questioning her ability to ever be able to try again. The fear of her loss confining her to infertility, she couldn't move on.

It was apparent that she was still reeling from the pregnancy, and she was consumed with finding justification for her loss. Desperately hoping for an answer beyond unfairness and these things just happen. She asked me over and over again, how did you keep going, how do you rectify something like this? I'd never truly thought about it before. The subsequent birth of my children had allowed me to leave infertility behind, never thinking to look back on my escape. The frantic desolation written all over her face was as familiar to me as my own. I felt like I was looking at a mirror image of myself from years before, furiously looking for answers, knowing that none were to be found.

I wanted to reach out and hug her, hug this broken, scared former version of myself. It had been years since my treatments, but looking at Julia I could still feel it all. It was as if I was visiting an old friend, one who was toxic and unhealthy and no matter how hard I tried to shake her, she always managed to come back around. I understood her manic need for answers, the preoccupation providing just enough chatter to quiet the fear slowly brewing inside. As long as I was active with my infertility I felt like I could cope, and I spent years trying to trick myself into believing that I had some control over my ability to conceive. Julia was still searching, not yet schooled in the game of denial that is a prerequisite for surviving infertility. Looking at her, her face so eager for answers, clinging with hope that I could help her, how could I tell her I lied? That I lied to myself and everyone around me by repeatedly telling myself it would all be okay? That was my big secret, pretend that everything is fine and it will be. The uncertainty of infertility wreaks havoc on your emotions and you have to give up trying to control something you clearly can't change. In reality, I never got through anything; I just gave up and blindly moved forward.

I shared with Julia about my experience with Nikki and how her brush with cancer helped put a new perspective on my dealings with infertility. It was at this point I realized I couldn't force anything. I had to trust that I was doing the best I could, and recognize that it was enough. I told her about Nikki's socks, how I used to wear them as a reminder to be grateful for the life that I had, and how they helped me during my darkest moment with infertility. As we were talking, I looked down and noticed I happened to be wearing Nikki's special socks. Impulsively, I pulled them off and handed a relative stranger my dirty socks. I told her to wear them when she needed a reminder her that her story would have its own happy ending, she just had to give it a chance to get there.

The timing of our eventual meeting was ironic because I was coming down from a pregnancy scare of my own. Surprisingly, for the first time in my life it had nothing to do with spotting or a low heart beat, I had thought I was pregnant. After years of doing nothing but tracking my cycle, I had apparently forgotten how to. I sat with a sense of déjà vu as I counted the days on my calendar only to find myself experiencing a completely new form of pregnancy related panic. Of all people, how could I have forgotten such an important detail as ovulation?

When making the decision to become parents, Peter and I hadn't planned much further than the delivery room. My three-month maternity leave had somehow morphed into six years, leaving Peter to shoulder the family's financial responsibility on his own. This was never intended to be a permanent leave for me, and we always assumed that at some point I'd go back to work. Having another baby would put that on hold for at least three more years. What would Peter say? Would he be angry? What about me, could I handle another round of diapers and an even bigger gap on my resume? Would I ever get back to the person I was before, or is this Mom person who I really was supposed to be?

I eventually got my period and a refresher course in birth control. More surprising than the pregnancy scare was my initial reaction. For the first time, I didn't associate a pregnancy with loss. I had thought about the implications of having another child, not another miscarriage. I had looked at the pregnancy as a whole and what it would mean to my family. All of my feelings about the pregnancy were external, based around my age and the financial ramifications of raising another child. I finally had a healthy reaction to a pregnancy and I couldn't believe it.

Julia contacted me recently. She was pregnant and had worn the socks to all of her appointments. Her new fear was labor and she was going to wear them during delivery. Once again I was looking at that other version of myself, someone who wouldn't let their fear stop them from proving statistics wrong, and was happily on their path to motherhood.

Rectifying is a personal choice. How do you rectify something that you can't control? There are so many paths to parenthood and all of the problems and pain encountered along the way ultimately become part of the solution. When I look at my children I don't see the losses that preceded them. Instead I see how lucky I am that these are the two that made it. I wouldn't wish infertility on anyone, but working so hard to be a parent helped make me a better one. I am more patient and forgiving knowing what it took to be in the position that I am. I have two children who want and love me and I couldn't ask for anything more than that.

Some people may continue trudging along through the uncertainty of infertility, and others may opt for adoption or childless living. It's not until you come to that decision, and the ultimate peace that comes with it, that you can rectify anything. I look at my miscarriages as a gift; they brought me the family I have. This last, almost pregnancy was also a gift. Paired with meeting Julia, I realize just how far I have come. I went from being a hopeless, angry, woman back to the happy person that had disappeared for so many years. I am healthy and have come full circle. I look at my kids and can't help but think yes, I can rectify anything. And it was worth it all.

Resources

(ABORM) The American Board of Oriental Medicine —
www.aborm.org

Acufinder (Acupuncture referral service) —
www.acufinder.com

AFA, American Fertility Association (Infertility and Family Building) —
www.theafa.org

The American Pregnancy Association —
www.americanpregnancy.org

The American Society for Reproductive Medicine —
www.asrm.org

RESOLVE, The National Infertility Association —
www.resolve.org

Acknowledgements

So many people helped inspire and encourage me while writing this book. I am so grateful for everyone's support and would especially like to thank Susan and Anastasios Miserlis. Without my *Wonderful Writing Wednesdays* (and many days in-between) I never would have been able to complete this book. Your support and love means so much to me and I am lucky to have you as parents. I have to thank my selfless husband Peter for letting me air out our dirty laundry and talk publicly about his privates. I owe you. To my siblings, Kevin, JP, Cecily, Theo, Mina, and Stacy, thank you for always being there and for being the inspiration for giving Theo a sister. You are all wonderful and deeply loved. To my father who probably thinks this book is about feminism, I love you and won't expect you to read any further than these acknowledgements.

To Tao my editor, despite your claim at not having any experience with infertility, you sure know how to write about it. Thank you for your editing expertise and willingness to say yes (even if Nikki wouldn't let you say no). To my dear friend Tracy who began this journey with me. I loved our lunches and am so thankful to have you in my life. We never made it to Oprah, but at least it's in print! Nikki, I am so grateful that you always pick up the phone and of course for your socks (even if they are strapped into Teva's). Danielle, for your gift that was bigger than we could ever have anticipated. Kelli, for your forgiveness and fabulousness.

To my oldest and dearest friend Athena, thank you for introducing me to yoga at a time when I needed it most, Namaste my friend. Christy, for San Francisco, you will forever be the baby Gandhi. To my biggest fans, Liza, Lara, Patsy and Karie, thank you for telling me to write a book and always asking for more. To my neighbor Eric, a million thanks for pulling my book out of cyberspace not once, but twice. And of course to Jeneanne for your kindness and yes, you are right, this is bigger than money.

Last but not least, to all the members of the Fertility Follies Reading Group and those of you who email me with stories of your own, this book is for you. Statistics lie and apparently a 5 percent chance is still a pretty good one. I wish you all a happy ending of your own.

– Erin

About the Author

Erin Miserlis has spent the better part of the past decade impersonating a guinea pig. Although no longer suffering from infertility, she still has the occasional post-traumatic hot flash. Erin holds a degree in psychology and a master's in human services administration, which she only uses to control her family. She resides in San Diego, California with her extremely patient husband and their two wild, miracle children. Erin writes a column on issues pertaining to infertility and miscarriage for the Examiner.com and can be followed on Facebook and Twitter.

You can contact Erin or learn more about *Fertility Follies, Adventures in Hormones & Hot Flashes* by visiting her website at: **www.fertilityfollies.com**